Ur and Uruk: The History and Legacy of the Ancient Sumerians' Two Most Important Cities

By Charles River Editors

Marcus Cyron's picture of part the front of the Inanna temple of the Kara Indasch from Uruk

About Charles River Editors

Charles River Editors is a boutique digital publishing company, specializing in bringing history back to life with educational and engaging books on a wide range of topics. Keep up to date with our new and free offerings with this 5 second sign up on our weekly mailing list, and visit Our Kindle Author Page to see other recently published Kindle titles.

We make these books for you and always want to know our readers' opinions, so we encourage you to leave reviews and look forward to publishing new and exciting titles each week.

Introduction

A 2008 picture of part of Uruk

Uruk

"And a river went out of Eden to water the garden; and from thence it was parted, and became into four heads. The name of the first is Pison...And the name of the second river is Gihon...And the name of the third river is Tigris: that is it which goeth toward the east of Assyria. And the fourth river is Euphrates. And the Lord God took the man, and put him into the Garden of Eden to dress it and to keep it." - Genesis 2: 10-15

In southern Iraq, a crushing silence hangs over the dunes. For nearly 5,000 years, the sands of the Iraqi desert have held the remains of the oldest known civilization: the Sumerians. When American archaeologists discovered a collection of cuneiform tablets in Iraq in the late 19th century, they were confronted with a language and a people who were at the time only scarcely known to even the most knowledgeable scholars of ancient Mesopotamia. The exploits and achievements of other Mesopotamian peoples, such as the Assyrians and Babylonians, were already known to a large segment of the population through the Old Testament and the nascent field of Near Eastern studies had unraveled the enigma of the Akkadian language that was widely used throughout the region in ancient times, but the discovery of the Sumerian tablets brought to light the existence of the Sumerian culture, which was the oldest of all the

Mesopotamian cultures.

Although the Sumerians continue to get second or even third billing compared to the Babylonians and Assyrians, perhaps because they never built an empire as great as the Assyrians or established a city as enduring and great as Babylon, they were the people who provided the template of civilization that all later Mesopotamians built upon. The Sumerians are credited with being the first people to invent writing, libraries, cities, and schools in Mesopotamia (Ziskind 1972, 34), and many would argue that they were the first people to create and do those things anywhere in world.

For a people so great it is unfortunate that their accomplishments and contributions, not only to Mesopotamian civilization but to civilization in general, largely go unnoticed by the majority of the public. Perhaps the Sumerians were victims of their own success; they gradually entered the historical record, established a fine civilization, and then slowly submerged into the cultural patchwork of their surroundings. They also never suffered a great and sudden collapse like other peoples of the ancient Near East, such as the Hittites, Assyrians and Neo-Babylonians did. A close examination of Sumerian culture and chronology reveals that the Sumerians set the cultural tone in Mesopotamia for several centuries in the realms of politics/governments, arts, literature, and religion. The Sumerians were truly a great people whose legacy continued long after they were gone.

Even today, the world owes the Sumerians a tremendous amount. When Western Europe was still in the Stone Age, it was the Sumerians who invented writing and the wheel, divided time into minutes and seconds, tamed nature, and built gigantic cities. They embraced culture and the arts, and their caravans crossed the desert, opening up the first trade routes. Their myths and legends inspired various origin stories, and their memory lives on in the Old Testament. They wrote the history of the birth of mankind. The heritage of the Sumerian civilization and their successors is everywhere.

No site better represents the importance of the Sumerians than the city of Uruk. Between the fourth and the third millennium BCE, Uruk was one of several city-states in the land of Sumer, located in the southern end of the Fertile Crescent, between the two great rivers of the Tigris and the Euphrates. Discovered in the late 19th century by the British archaeologist William Loftus, it is this site that has revealed much of what is now known of the Sumerian, Akkadian, and Neo-Sumerian people.

Although Uruk was not the only city that the Sumerians built during the Uruk period, it was by far the greatest and also the source of most of the archeological and written evidence concerning early Sumerian culture (Kuhrt 2010, 1:23). Uruk went from being the world's first major city to the most important political and cultural center in the ancient Near East in relatively quick fashion. Around 3200 BCE, the Sumerian Uruk culture began to expand beyond the borders of Sumer, which coincided with the emergence of writing (Kuhrt 2010, 1:23). The form of writing that the Sumerians developed became known by its Greek name, "cuneiform," for the wedge style characters that it employed (van de Mieroop 2007, 28). Writing, like many other inventions throughout world history, appears to have been created because of necessity; as the Uruk culture grew, the Sumerians needed to develop a sophisticated form of record keeping, which could only have been done through writing (van de Mieroop 2007, 28). Despite being used exclusively for the Sumerian language at first, the cuneiform writing system was later adapted and used by a number of different languages in the ancient Near East such as the following: Akkadian, Hittite, and Old Persian (Dalby 1986, 475).

Ur

A picture of soldiers walking among the ruins of Ur

Long before Alexandria was a city and even before Memphis and Babylon had attained greatness, the ancient Mesopotamian city of Ur stood foremost among ancient Near Eastern cities. Today, the greatness and cultural influence of Ur has been largely forgotten by most people, partially because its monuments have not stood the test of time the way other ancient culture's monuments have. For instance, the monuments of Egypt were made of stone while those of Ur and most other Mesopotamian cities were made of mud brick and as will be discussed in this report, mud-brick may be an easier material to work with than stone but it also decays much quicker. The same is true to a certain extent for the written documents that were produced at Ur.

Despite the ephemeral nature of its monuments and to some extent its written texts, Ur proved to be an inspiration to the Sumerians who built the city and also to later cultures and dynasties that inhabited Mesopotamia. An examination of primary sources relating to Ur, as well as archaeological excavations done in the ancient city reveal that the city was a cultural beacon for thousands of years. Ur began as a Sumerian city of secondary importance but quickly grew to be the most important Sumerian city.

At its height Ur was the center of a great dynasty that controlled most of Mesopotamia directly through a well maintained army and bureaucracy and the areas that were not under its direct control were influenced by Ur's diplomats and religious ideas. This study will also reveal that Ur was a truly resilient city because it survived the downfall of the Sumerians, outright destruction at the hands of the Elamites, and later occupations by numerous other peoples, which included Saddam Hussein more recently. Ur inspired the imaginations of ancient peoples, but it has also enraptured the minds of moderns, who have worked for over 150 years to unlock the city's mysteries. Truly, when it comes to important ancient cities, Ur should be counted among the greatest.

Ur and Uruk: The History and Legacy of the Ancient Sumerians' Two Most Important Cities traces the history and legacy of two of the most influential cities of antiquity. Along with pictures of important people, places, and events, you will learn about the history of Uruk and Ur like never before, in no time at all.

Ur and Uruk: The History and Legacy of the Ancient Sumerians' Two Most Important Cities
About Charles River Editors
Introduction
Uruk
   The Sumerian Origins of Uruk
   Contemporary Origin Stories
   The Foundations of a Primeval City
   A Bird's Eye View of Uruk
   Religion and Power
   Innovation in Uruk
   Cuneiform Writing
   Trade Routes
   The Spread of Uruk Culture
   Jemdet Nasr and the Early Dynastic Periods
   The Fall of Uruk
   Archaeological Work
Ur
   Chapter 1: An Inspiration for Mesopotamia
   Chapter 2: The Modern Discovery of Ur
   Chapter 3: Ur and the Early Dynastic Period (ca. 2900-2500 BCE)
   Chapter 4: Ur during the Third Dynasty of Ur (2112-2004 BCE)
   Chapter 5: Other Monuments and Events at Ur during the Ur III Dynasty
   Chapter 6: The End of the Ur III Dynasty and the Temporary Destruction of Ur
   Chapter 7: Ur's Revival under the Kassites and Babylonians
   Chapter 8: The Assyrians and Ur
   Chapter 9: Ur in Later Ancient Times
   Chapter 10: Ur's Modern Struggle for Existence
   Online Resources
   Bibliography
Free Books by Charles River Editors
Discounted Books by Charles River Editors

Uruk

The Sumerian Origins of Uruk

The harsh climate of southern Iraq has not changed for thousands of years, yet men and women once lived there. Sandwiched between the Mediterranean and the Persian Gulf is the region that the Greek historian Polybius called Mesopotamia–"the country between two rivers." This refers to the stretch of land between the Tigris in the east and the Euphrates in the west. [1]

Both the Tigris and Euphrates rise from the mountains of Armenia, fed by melting snow from the high plateaus. The rivers tumble down the mountain slopes, bringing with them tons of silt as they pick up speed. In ancient times, the Tigris and the Euphrates ran through much of Mesopotamia as a single river, separating downstream from Nippur. They run parallel for more than two thousand kilometers before they merge to form the Shatt al-Arab waterway. The rivers become calmer at this point as they travel through the wide desert plains to the south. There, they deposit fertile soil onto their banks, all the way to the Persian Gulf. On each side of the Shatt al-Arab, an agricultural landscape prospered.[2]

Water was not only important for farming and drinking; it was also vital for quick transport across the region, facilitating trade and communication. The Tigris is a fast-flowing river, passing through the Syrian uplands before it branches into a number of channels on the Mesopotamian plains. This was a very difficult river to cross throughout history, with very few points north of present-day Mosul where it could be safely forded. The Euphrates has much lower banks, and could be used by ships, and the floodplains on either side of the river were suitable for irrigation.

In a place like Mesopotamia, which had land for agriculture but was short of many other vital resources such as wood, stone, and metal-bearing ores, these water-based networks became the preferred means of trading between complementary economic spheres, but the waterways could also be a terrible adversary. Each year, spring floods would sweep away everything in their path, leading many to wonder why anyone would settle in an area so vulnerable to the forces of nature.

An investigation of ancient Mesopotamia must accept that the communities that live there were inextricably entangled with the environment and landscape of which they were a part. There are four main ecological zones in the ancient Near East.[3] First, there are the chains of high mountains that frame ancient Mesopotamia, such as the ancient and brooding Zagros Mountain range. The tallest of these are between three and five thousand meters above sea level, with

---

[1] Polybius (2012) *Polybius: The Histories*. Chicago: University of Chicago
[2] Wilkinson, T. J. (2000) "Regional approaches to Mesopotamian archaeology: the contribution of archaeological surveys." *Journal of Archaeological Research*, 8:3. 219–267. .
[3] Bahrani, Z. (1998) "Conjuring Mesopotamia: Imaginative Geography a World Past." in Meskell, L. *Archaeology under Fire: Nationalism, Politics and Heritage in the Eastern Mediterranean and Middle East*. London: Routledge. 159–174

several reaching over nine thousand feet in height, the tallest being Zard Kuh at a height of thirteen thousand, eight hundred feet. Most were heavily forested during the time of the Sumerians, with cold and wet winters and warm summers. Although the Zagros mountain range separates the lands of Mesopotamia from lands farther east, these mighty mountains did not act as absolute boundaries, but rather, zones of integration and fragmentation.[4] To the far north, bordering the mountainous ranges of Cappadocia and the Caucasus, is a well-watered and fertile region that was the land of ancient Assyria, focused on the capital city of Ashur, and in the eastern region of the Zagros Mountains is the ancient land of Elam, focused on the area known as Khuzistan.

Next is a zone of foothills and grasslands, with warm and dry summers and temperate winters, such as the areas around the Eastern Mediterranean, Anatolia, and the Beqaa Valley of eastern Lebanon. The climate and soil of these regions has historically allowed the cultivation of cereals, and it was here the earliest irrigation took place. Third is the steppe zone, with mild, dry winters and hot, dry summers. These expansive, treeless grasslands stretch across Eurasia, from the Anatolian Plateau in present-day Turkey, all the way to Western China. A fine example of this ecozone can be found in the area of land to the west of the Euphrates. Finally are the desert zones, with very hot summers and mild winters, which can be found across ancient Mesopotamia. To the west and southwest of Mesopotamia is the great Arabian Desert, separating the Fertile Crescent from the Arabian Peninsula.[5]

Sumer was located in central and southern Mesopotamia, where the Euphrates and the Tigris run close to one another. Here, the low hills and fertile plains of central Mesopotamia are followed south by a vast landscape of swamps, jungles, and countless streams and rivulets where the Euphrates and the Tigris delta into the Persian Gulf. Only barges are able to reach the heart of this maze of tall reeds.[6] This was the land of Sumer, and home to the earliest cities in Mesopotamia.

---

[4] Bahrani, 1998
[5] Bahrani, 1998
[6] Foster, B. R., and Polinger Foster, K. (2009) *Civilizations of Ancient Iraq*. Princeton: Princeton University Press. .

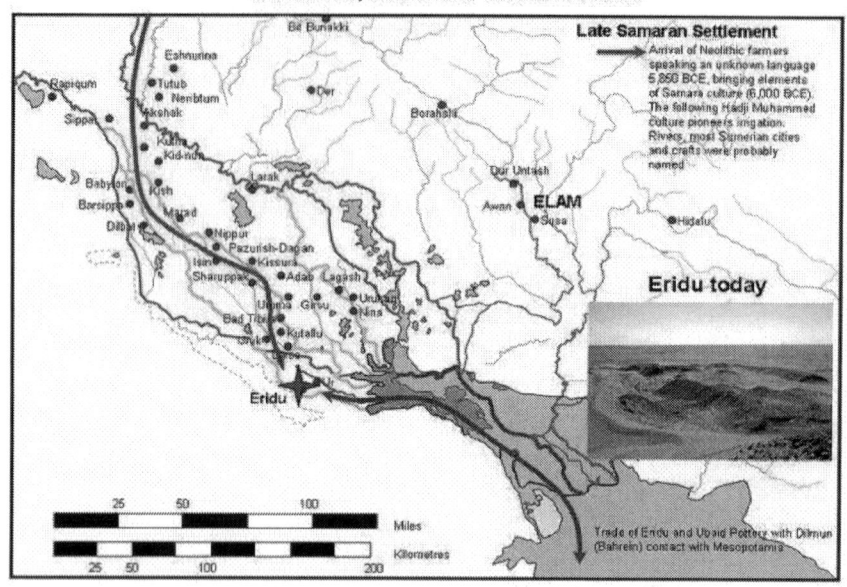

A map of the region during the early history of the Sumerians

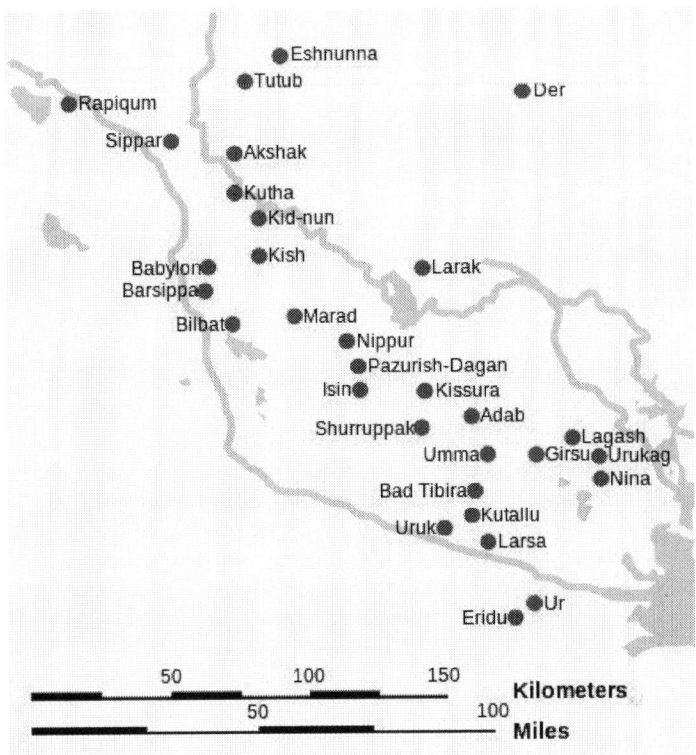

A map of Sumer

Climate was a major factor in the major sociopolitical upheavals that took place in the region during the period of the rise and fall of Uruk. The varied ecozones of Mesopotamia resulted in a diversity of flora and fauna important for the emergence of domestication and agriculture, and resources for trade. Archaeologists in Anatolia have solved one part of the puzzle regarding where the Sumerians have come from, and how they first decided to settle on the floodplains of the two rivers. People have lived at the crossroads of great migration routes on the fertile plateaus of Anatolia, several thousand kilometers from Mesopotamia, since time immemorial, and many of the same fruits and vegetables have existed and been traded around the region for thousands of years. In 1958, archaeologists discovered the nine thousand year old ruins of the village of Çayönü in Turkey.[7] Three thousand, five hundred years before Sumer, people settled

---

[7] Braidwood, R. J., Çambel, H., Redman, C. L., and Watson, P. J. (1972) "Beginnings of Village-Farming Communities in Southeastern Turkey." *Proceedings of the National Academy of Sciences*, 68:6. 1236 - 1240.

in this fertile land. They were an aceramic society, but they did make buildings of mud-brick walls upon dry stone foundations. Of even more importance was the Einkorn wheat found in the settlement, which was believed to have grown wild all over the hills, and which produced seeds that could be planted and stored by the ancient community. This grain could form an entire household's staple diet and could be stored for a great length of time, making it possible for large-scale population expansion and the foundation of civilizations.[8] It was this that allowed people to settle in one place–realizing they had a steady supply of food available, they remained where it was. It is unclear if this was an "accidental discovery" or the result of human observation and understanding, but this was how agriculture was born.[9]

With the spread of agriculture, people were able to store food for several weeks or months instead of being reliant on hunting animals every few days. Thanks to these successes in agriculture the population in ancient Mesopotamia grew as the first sedentary groups began to colonize the land along the flood plains of the two rivers.

The Ubaid period (approximately 6500 to 3800 BCE) is named after the Tell of al-Ubaid in southern Iraq, the earliest settlement on southern Mesopotamia's alluvial plain.[10] During this period, a number of vitally important technological advances were made by the people of Mesopotamia, including the adoption of the wheel and the beginning of the Chalcolithic period.[11] Moreover, the Ubaid represents the earliest urbanization to take place in Mesopotamia. These early urban landscapes were mostly found in the form of tell sites. A "tell" is the name given to an ancient city that has been buried over time, which in the present day resembles a mound composed of stacked layers of mud-brick architecture. The tell is almost entirely artificial, its height being the result of many generations of people occupying the site, building new structures upon that which existed before and rebuilding once again when the mud-brick buildings degrade. This results in sites of enormous temporal depth, represented by a complex stratigraphy that must be carefully excavated and analyzed by archaeologists to create the site's timeline.

The Sumerians became the dominant cultural group during this period. Irrigated food provided a steady supply to them, and as they dug ditches to divert channels of river water from the Tigris and Euphrates to the otherwise dry land, they turned the desert of southern Mesopotamia into a fertile delta. Their population rapidly grew with the resulting abundant food supply. Sumer was divided into several city-states of around two hundred thousand people each. Each city state was organized around the worship of a deity, whose home was the temple.[12] Ziggurats and other monumental structures were built at these sites, which were protected by tall fortified walls.

---

[8] Hopf, M., and Zohary, D. (2000) *Domestication of Plants in the Old World: The Origin and Spread of Cultivated Plants in West Asia, Europe, and the Nile Valley*. Oxford: Oxford University Press
[9] Hopf and Zohary, 2000. .
[10] Delougaz, P. (1938) "A Short Investigation of the Temple at Al-'Ubaid". *Iraq*, 5. 1 – 11
[11] Bogucki, P. (1990) *The Origins of Human Society*. Malden: Blackwell
[12] Lloyd, S. (1978) *The Archaeology of Mesopotamia: From the Old Stone Age to the Persian Conquest*. London: Thames and Hudson. .

The Sumerians invented a great many things, of which none was more important than the wheel, which they used for transport, farming, and the production of specialized ceramics. They were amongst the earliest to make use of writing, first through pictographs and later through cuneiform script.

One of the most prominent sites in southern Mesopotamia at this period was Ur, an immense city, located close to the ancient shoreline of the Persian Gulf. Ur was surrounded by four thousand hectares of cereal fields, built on the east bank of the Euphrates River. More than forty thousand people–mostly fishers and farmers–lived in the swampland surrounding the port city of Ur, and the city itself contained a population of up to thirty four thousand people.[13] The city was circled on all sides by a canal leading on to the Euphrates, with harbors to the west and north. Typical of many cities in Mesopotamia, the city of Ur was ringed by a mud-brick wall and dominated by the palace and a great ziggurat devoted to the main god of the city, Nanna, the god of the moon. Made of fired bricks that were covered in tar, the Ziggurat of Ur was built to last. It required an estimated five years and one thousand, five hundred workers to build its base alone.[14] The tall structure dominated the landscape, and farmers up to twenty kilometers away were able to see the household of their god.[15]

---

[13] Leick, G. (2001) *Mesopotamia: The invention of the city*. London: Allen Lane
[14] Woolley, C. L. and Moorey, P. R. S. (1982) *Ur of the Chaldees: Revised and Updated Edition of Sir Leonard Woolley's Excavations at Ur*. Cornell: Cornell University Press
[15] Leick, 2001

M. Lubinski's picture of the ruins of Ur

A picture of soldiers walking among the ruins of Ur

Long before Alexandria was a city and even before Memphis and Babylon had attained greatness, Ur stood foremost among ancient Near Eastern cities. Today, the greatness and cultural influence of Ur has been largely forgotten by most people, partially because its monuments have not stood the test of time the way other ancient culture's monuments have. For instance, the monuments of Egypt were made of stone while those of Ur and most other Mesopotamian cities were made of mud-brick and as will be discussed in this report, mud-brick may be an easier material to work with than stone but it also decays much quicker. The same is true to a certain extent for the written documents that were produced at Ur. The people of Mesopotamia, which Ur was part of, employed the cuneiform system of writing; since cuneiform was almost always written on clay tablets, modern scholars have been forced with the unfortunate problem that many of those tablets have been broken and made unreadable throughout the centuries. Despite the ephemeral nature of its monuments and to some extent its written texts, Ur proved to be an inspiration to the Sumerians who built the city and also to later cultures and dynasties that inhabited Mesopotamia.

Northern Mesopotamia also developed its own, local culture in the late Ubaid period, known as the Gawra Culture, represented by the archaeological site of Tepe Gawra. A round house discovered there by archaeologists digging in the early twentieth century contained evidence of storage spaces for grain and finely carved, stone, pear-shaped mace heads. A particularly splendid tiny wolf's head made of electrum (an alloy of gold and silver) was also found at this site, indicating the well-developed craft skills that existed at this time.[16] There is also evidence of extensive trade networks existing during this period that connected Tepe Gawra with other city-states around Mesopotamia and Eurasia, such as beads of lapis lazuli that were found at this site, the precious mineral being available only from Budakhshan province in northern Afghanistan, over two thousand kilometers away.[17]

Contemporary Origin Stories

The above chronology has been revealed through the careful study of material remains and documentary evidence by archaeologists and scholars. The Sumerian King List from this period acts as a framework for the study of Mesopotamian chronology. It lists the ancient kings of Sumer, the length of their reign, and the location of "official" kingship, but it also gives an invaluable perspective into contemporary understandings of their own chronology.[18] The textual record of Mesopotamia also offers us a glimpse into how contemporaries viewed their history. Many of these were recovered from the library of Nineveh, and George Smith, a 19th century Londoner, who studied Sumerian and worked at the British Museum, deciphered many cuneiform cylinders and tablets and revealed much about Sumerian myths and legends.

---

[16] Rothman, M. S. (2001) *Tepe Gawra: The Evolution of a Small, Prehistoric Center in Northern Iraq.* Pennsylvania: University Museum Publications. . .
[17] Herrmann, G. (1966) "Lapis Lazuli: The Early Phases of Its Trade." *Oxford University Dissertations*
[18] Young, D. W. (1991) "The Incredible Regnal Spans of Kish I in the Sumerian King List." *Journal of Near Eastern Studies*, 50: 1. 23 – 35

Smith

It was Smith who first discovered and translated the *Epic of Gilgamesh*, one of the oldest written works of literature. Many aspects of Eurasian civilization, and Christianity in particular, are steeped in the mythos of the ancient Mesopotamian world.[19]

According to the cuneiform texts, mighty gods walked the earth during the Antediluvian Age, in the time before the Great Flood. Growing apathetic and tired of their manual labor, the gods created humans to serve as their servants and slaves.[20] Before long, the gods had bred with the humans and the children of these unions had become demigods, ruling as god-kings over mankind for immensely long periods. Some of these kings that were described on the Sumerian

---

[19] Foster and Polinger, 2009
[20] Other contemporary legends describe an extremely long-lived race from the planet Nibiru, known as the Anunnaki (the "seven judges" or "those who came from Heaven to Earth"). This race is described as having bred with apes from Earth to create humans.

King List ruled for more than 64,000 years.[21]

After a period of time, humans had grown in number and become increasingly troublesome. The gods met in their city of Shuruppak–a site known also as Tell Fara on the banks of the Euphrates–where the supreme god En-Lil decided that mankind must be destroyed by a great flood.[22] One of the gods called Enki, also known as Ea, pleaded with En-Lil, but in vain. He decided to protect humankind by warning a man called Ziusudra of the impending disaster. Ziusudra built an ark, filing its holds with precious metals, grain seeds, and animals. He managed to get his family on board before the god of thunder, Adad, released the deluge upon the Earth. After six days and nights of storm, the world was submerged, but on the seventh day, the storm abated.

---

[21] Young, 1991
[22] Ristvet, L. (2014) *Ritual, Performance, and Politics in the Ancient Near East.* Cambridge: Cambridge University Press.

The part of the epic describing the deluge

Osama Shukir Muhammed Amin's picture of another tablet from the epic

After the flood, the gods realized their actions had been rash, as it was the work and worship of humans that allowed the deities to live their leisurely lives. On the seventh day, Ziusudra released a dove that, finding no resting place, returned to him. On the eighth day, he released a raven that never returned, meaning it had found dry land, and mankind was saved. The gods were delighted to find that Ziusudra had survived the flood and made him an immortal demigod. Ziusudra's children returned to Sumer, and over time, began to breed and multiply once more.[23]

---

[23] Ristvet, 2014

However, little changed regarding the lawless manners of the people until a mythical sage known as Adapa came to Sumer and taught them about the arts, sciences, writing, and other aspects of civilization. Humans learned how to build cities, to construct temples and other monumental structures, to compile and enforce laws, and to master the sciences, geometry, and mathematics. During this time, Eridu, the First City of the god Enki, was founded under the guidance of Adapa, who became the city's first priest-king.[24]

Soon thereafter, Adapa returned to the sea, but six other sages like him appeared and dwelled in Eridu, teaching human initiates wisdom and science that had been lost in the flood.[25] After Eridu, a number of other city-states were founded in the land of Sumer, including Kish, Larsa, Nippur, Sippar, Ur, and Uruk.

The Foundations of a Primeval City

Extensive regional surveys carried out by archaeologists in the 1960s have revealed the largest city in Mesopotamia, dating from between the fourth and the third millenniums BCE, to be Uruk, a site located approximately 100 kilometers northwest of Ur. Uruk was occupied for more than five thousand years (from the early Ubaid period to the third century CE), and by the third millennium BCE, this city had expanded over an area of approximately four thousand hectares.[26]

Archaeologists define a "city" in the context of ancient Mesopotamia as a constructed landscape. Through inferences and comparisons with modern states, a successful ancient Mesopotamian city is said to have the following characteristics:[27] it contains evidence of a stratified and hierarchical society, with a centralized authority that is simultaneously dependent on the accumulation of resources by its population, and the suppression of its competitors. A vast hinterland is required to supply the urban population with food and trade systems are established to acquire resources that are not locally available. It exhibits evidence of specialized, and often standardized, crafts, as well as monumental statements of centralized planning and communal (if not consensual) effort. The ancient and magnificent city of Uruk exhibits all of these characteristics.

Like other Mesopotamian city-states, Uruk consisted of the city itself and a vast hinterland, surrounding it on all sides. This contained the arable land filled with canals and irrigation channels, as well as a number of satellite towns and smaller settlements. Subsistence in the region was reliant on irrigation-based agriculture. Unlike areas where crops could grow without supervision, with less than three hundred millimeters of mean annual precipitation, farming could only be done around Uruk by carefully managing the irrigation of the land according to a method known as "sharouf," which is still used to the present day. Both the Tigris and Euphrates

---

[24] Young, 1991
[25] Green, M. W. (1975) *Eridu in Sumerian Literature*. Chicago: University of Chicago
[26] Rothman, M. S. (2001b) *Uruk, Mesopotamia & Its Neighbors*. Santa Fe: School of American Research Press. .
[27] Leick, 2001

were prone to violent, unpredictable floods that spilled over their banks. This more often washed fields away, rather than replenishing them, and the cycle of floods and rains, planting and harvest, would have provided a framework that governed life as a farmer at Uruk.

The emergence of ceremonial monument building in southern Mesopotamia is thought to be the impetus that sparked urban development (Kuhrt 2010, 1:25). Temples were believed to be the house of the patron deity of a particular city so goods were often received and distributed at the temple complex (van de Mieroop 2007, 24). By the late Uruk period, temples were by far the largest buildings in any city and were constructed at great cost in material resources and labor (van de Mieroop 2007, 24). As the size and importance of temples grew in Sumer during the Uruk period, the building and architectural techniques also evolved.

The Sumerians developed the standard for Mesopotamian temple architecture during the Ubaid period and subsequent ethnic groups would follow that template through the Hellenistic period. One architectural technique that the Sumerians developed, which was used in all later periods in Mesopotamian history, was the buttresses and recessed walls (Frankfort 1996, 18). The evolution of the Mesopotamian temple complex then finally moved towards its final expression – the ziggurat. Beginning in the Uruk period the temple complex began to include a tower on a platform, known as a ziggurat (Frankfort 1996, 20). The "White Temple" at Uruk had an "archaic" ziggurat that rose about forty feet above the ground, which was enough to dominate the featureless countryside for miles around (Frankfort 1996, 20). To the Sumerians the ziggurat represented a mountain on top of which was the particular deity's abode who the temple was dedicated (Frankfort 1996, 21). In later more literate periods of Mesopotamian history the names of the ziggurats were recorded in writing, which indicates the theological importance of the structures. For instance, the ziggurat of the god Enlil was known as "House of the Mountain, Mountain of the Storm, and Bond Between Heaven and Earth" (Frankfort 1996, 22). The materials needed to build these great structures had to be imported from long distances to Uruk, which indicates that the early Sumerian city was not just an important cultural center, but also a political hub.

Today, scholars often refer to the late Uruk period as the "Uruk Expansion" because it was a period when the city of Uruk exercised immense influence not only throughout Mesopotamia, but also in neighboring regions of the ancient Near East. In fact, one may argue that the Sumerians of the late Uruk period created the world's first empire. The expansion of Uruk's influence was directly related to its need for resources not found in southern Mesopotamia, so the Sumerians monopolized trade networks that brought such commodities as stone, timber, and lapis lazuli to Sumer. Although the Sumerians were literate by the late Uruk period, the records are still minimal in number and the best archaeological information of the expansion process actually comes from outlying regions – such as western Iran, northern Syria, and southern Turkey – that were influenced by Uruk (van de Mieroop 2007, 35).

When they built cities like Uruk, the Mesopotamians were shaping the world in their own image. This relationship can be seen on an alabaster vase, more than one meter high, discovered in Uruk during excavations in 1933. Known today as the Warka Vase, the low-relief images displayed on its exterior depict the Sumerians' gratitude toward nature. The cereals and animals are depicted as ears of wheat and herds of sheep.[28] The image also expresses their religious fervor in its depiction of a procession of men bearing offerings as they approach the sanctuary of Inanna–the goddess of heaven and earth.

---

[28] Ristvet, 2014

Einsamer Schütze's picture of a replica of the Warka Vase

The members of the procession of the Warka Vase are met by the high priest clad in robes, indicating the social stratification taking place at the city.[29] Mesopotamian society was organized in a highly hierarchical manner. At the top was the priest-king, who claimed divine authority over his subjects. An elite class existed beneath him, consisting of nobles, priests, scribes, bureaucratic officials, and warriors. There would have been a wide range of merchants, traders, and artisans in the city. The remainder of the population, and by far the majority, were serfs and slaves, tasked with all manual labor.[30]

The vase is the earliest representation of such a scene in Mesopotamian art, and it influenced similar scenes that were often depicted on reliefs of royal palaces through the Neo-Assyrian period. Another artistic style that appears to have been first developed by the Sumerians during the Uruk period, which was replicated centuries later by the Assyrians, was the royal lion hunt motif (Kuhrt 2010: 1:23). On one particular stela, which was housed in the National Museum of Baghdad, a hunter dressed in possibly royal garb hunts lions with a bow (Frankfort 1996, 33). It may be that the lion hunt scene from Uruk is a commemoration of a marshland reclamation project (Frankfort 1996, 34), but the badly damaged relief is not accompanied with a text so it is not for certain if the scene was meant to depict an actual event or if it belonged in a religious or ritual context, which would mean that scene would have a more symbolic or metaphorical meaning. Whatever the purpose, it is hard to ignore a possible Sumerian influence on the numerous lion hunt scenes that Assyrian king Ashurbanipal (668-627 BCE) adorned his palace with nearly two and half thousand years later (Curtis and Reade 1995, 84-89).

A Bird's Eye View of Uruk

Uruk developed in a series of stages over time and the layout of the city was vastly different in the fourth millennium when compared to its state under Akkadian and Babylonian rule. To give a general sense of the layout of the city, it can be described as an immense urban landscape, surrounded by four thousand hectares of cereal fields, built on the southwestern bank of the Euphrates River. Typical of many cities in Mesopotamia, the city of Uruk was ringed by a mud-brick wall, believed to have been built under Gilgamesh, the legendary king of Uruk. The area it enclosed is believed to have contained a population of between fifty and eighty thousand people.

Behind the high city wall was a warren of narrow, winding streets and courtyard houses, haphazardly distributed according to social class and profession. Three-story buildings jostled for space with single-story ones. None of the houses were aligned according to any top-down ground plan, other than that which was provided by the incredible network of canals piercing through the landscape, drawing fresh water from the Euphrates. Most of the serfs and slaves in the city lived in this sprawling maze of buildings, the facades of which had no openings other than low doors for access and a few air vents. With the frequent dust storms in the region, large window spaces were inconvenient, and people often slept on their rooftops, which were much cooler at night

---

[29] Ristvet, 2014
[30] Crawford, H. E. W. (2004) *Sumer and the Sumerians.* Cambridge: Cambridge University Press

than the small rooms of their houses.

From its earliest times, daily life in Uruk was centered on the temples in the Eanna Precincts and the Anu Precinct. People prayed and worshiped there and political and economic decisions were made by the elite and bureaucratic classes of the city that operated there. Uruk is believed to have originally formed when two smaller settlements grew to the extent that they merged, and cores of these original settlements became the two temple areas of the city. Both of these temples contained the standard furnishings of a Sumerian temple, namely, an offering table and an altar to the deity.[31] Also located within the temple area were the quarters of the city's scribes and priests.

Carmen Ansinsio's picture of the ruins of the Temple of Inanna

One of the finest monumental landscapes in the city was located in Eanna Precinct This vast complex was composed of a number of structures, great buildings with colonnaded courtyards, various temples made of precious limestone devoted to Inanna, goddess of fertility, and structures decorated with mosaics of riemchen, square sectioned brick cones with colored heads arranged in the colorful manner that become typically characteristic of the Uruk culture.

The other major religious center of the ancient city was Anu Precinct, which contained the temple of An, god of the sky. The complex was dominated by the ziggurat, accessed by a

---

[31] Ristvet, 2014

monumental processional staircase leading up to the central altar. Located close to the altar was the so-called "White Temple," a well-preserved structure (which is rare for the area) with a cardinally oriented central hall and stepped altar. This gleaming white temple had whitewashed walls that would have gleamed in the bright, Iraqi sunlight. Reaching a height of thirteen meters, the size and complexity of its architecture is testament to the fact that this building was constructed with the intention of impressing the population of the city and its hinterland, while evoking the wealth and power of those who had commissioned it.[32]

The structures of the city were almost entirely made of mud-brick, a material that degrades quickly, so the old structures of each previous generation would have to have been torn down and replaced by fresh buildings. Garbage was either burned or simply left on the road outside of homes. Over time, layer upon layer of the city's garbage and ancient structures caused the entire urban site to rise above the lowlands.[33]

The monumental temple districts experienced the same trend of leveling of what was there before and the rebuilding of something new. These successive falls and restorations became part of the elite psyche, as future generations were encouraged, through foundation inscriptions, to restore inscribed names, stele, and clay inscriptions.

Religion and Power

The Sumerians' religious sensibilities are not easy to comprehend. Archaeologists have found temples, texts full of myths, and bas reliefs showing rituals, but the deeper numinous feelings and cosmological perspectives are not well understood to this day. There is an obvious sense of divine power, and it is clear that the Sumerians believed there were forces which humans had to serve, and with whom they had to come to terms. Their religion was one of servitude and prayer, but through service to the gods, they ensured that life in the hostile environment ran smoothly.[34]

The gods instilled fear and respect, symbolizing the Sumerians' mistrust of nature. Since nothing in ancient Mesopotamia happened without divine consent or intervention, a collapsing empire must have meant the Sumerians were guilty of upsetting the gods. Hundreds of gods were worshipped in Uruk and wider Mesopotamia, and there appeared to be considerable religious tolerance, as pantheons between these groups were shared and merged. The prestige of the gods was considered dependent on the fortunes of the home city, with each divinity in the Mesopotamian pantheon playing a role, and each one ruling over a city. En-Lil, god of air and earth, ruled over the city of Nippur. Udu, god of justice and truth, was worshipped in Larsa. Enki, god of water and the world, was worshipped in Eridu. Nanna, the god of the moon, was the patron deity of Ur. Each city's name was derived from the god's name in classical Sumerian:

---

[32] Rothman, 2001
[33] Castel, C. and Peltenburg, E. (2006) Urbanism on the margins: third millennium BC Al-Rawda in the arid zone of Syria. *Antiquity*, 81. 601 - 616
[34] Ristvet, 2014

"Urim." Other deities were worshipped in the lesser temples around the city.[35] Inanna, known to the Babylonians as the fertility goddess Ishtar, to the Greeks as Aphrodite, and to the Romans as Venus, was worshiped in Uruk. She is believed to have inspired both love and war.

Rulers considered themselves to be agents of the gods. Their roles included performing ceremonies to ward off evil and gain the good will of their deities, which took place in temples, sacred groves, and hilltops, all significant places in the landscape. Sacrifices were often a regular part of such ritual ceremonies, alongside the taking of libations such as beer, water, wine, and oil, collected by a bureaucratic administration for that specific purpose.

A class of religious bureaucrats controlled the political and economic life of Uruk in the name of these god-kings. Scribes recorded the hopes of the Sumerians, the texts of which have survived in the archives of the city. In exchange for their virtue, devotion, and respect for the established order, the people of Uruk hoped for eternal life in the next world.

The upkeep of temples and organization of ceremonies required a large body of priests and other staff. Every day, people brought offerings of celestial food to the gods (which later fed the temple's priests and staff). The archives describe the daily meal of its four main gods as follows: two hundred and fifty loaves of bread, one thousand cakes, fifty sheep, eight lambs, two oxen, and one calf.[36] It was through this complex and centralized bureaucracy that large numbers of people could be drawn together to work on the city's massive building works. Priests and scribes were used to organize engineering works requiring hundreds and thousands of laborers. This extended beyond the city walls, in the construction and maintenance of the irrigation canals, upon which the population's existence depended.

Innovation in Uruk

In ancient Mesopotamia, the balance between man and nature could easily tip against the former. The secret of Sumerian success lay in their ability to tame the unpredictable sources of water that existed in their lands. To take control of their water, they invented the wheel, dug many hundreds of kilometers of canals, reservoirs, and dams for their irrigation, and in doing so, managed to subdue and harness the turbulent waters of the Tigris and the Euphrates for their own use.

As they set about mastering their new discovery, these early farmers invented many tools. Grain was the main source of wealth for all classes in the city, and their main preoccupation was to find ways to boost the production of crops. Clay tablets recovered by archaeologists depict a device used to make sowing seeds more economical. The seeds would be deposited via a funnel that ensured regular and even distribution in the furrows. Sumerians grew bountiful crops and Uruk was surrounded by hundreds of thousands of hectares of fertilized landscape. In some

---

[35] Ristvet, 2014
[36] Ristvet, 2014

areas, wheat, millet, and barley could be harvested twice a year.[37]

By examining the social practice of alcohol consumption, which increased in Mesopotamia through the fourth and third millennia, and studying the association between drinking paraphernalia and social behavior, historians can see the process of growing social stratification. Alcohol was utilized as a useful medium that allowed surplus agricultural produce to be converted into labor, prestige, and political power, creating a useful and socially valued material that could be exploited by the emerging bureaucratic elite.

The Mesopotamian evolution of a large range of competing or complementary economic institutions in the urban environment created a stratification of recognized social contexts in which drinking took place.[38] Each of these had their own etiquette and use of vessel type, from the high-stemmed wheel-thrown bowls found at Arslantepe[39] to consumption from large storage vessels through straws found in elite burials in southern Mesopotamia.[40] Alcohol was very useful for the rising bureaucracy in complex societies like Uruk. Rival elites could make use of the conspicuous consumption of alcohol to secure their identity as providers, attract followers, reward success, reinforce loyalty, and support budding specialists.[41] Specialization in the production of alcoholic beverages is seen in the variety of the sizes of vessels, types of beer, and ceramic evidence for the distillation of liquids, as well as large-scale production sites, such as those at Abu Salabikh and Khafaje.[42] At the Uruk highland enclave of Godin Tepe, archaeologists discovered the presence of wine and beer products at the center of the complex, manufactured and distributed along with other food products by an official bureaucracy.[43]

The Sumerians also made use of standardized units of length, area, and capacity measurement.[44] They had separate units for measuring barley, malt, wheat, beer, milk, fish, dead and alive animals, and slaves. The standard unit of capacity was the *sila*, which was the volume of a single, beveled-rim bowl. Weight was measured in *shekels*, which weighed about the same as a modern pound, or about half a kilogram. Coins were not used in Mesopotamia, though the existence of standardized weights for silver serve as measures of value and indicate its use as a means of exchange.[45]

In studying the beveled-rim bowl category, it's possible to see how the manufacturing,

---

[37] Crawford, 2004
[38] Douglas, M. (1987) *Constructive drinking: perspectives on drink from anthropology.* Cambridge: Cambridge University Press
[39] Frangipane, M. (1997)"A 4th-millenium temple/palace complex at Arslantepe-Malatya. North-South relations and the formation of early state societies in the Northern regions of Greater Mesopotamia." *Paléorient*, 23:1. 45-73
[40] Joffe, A.H. (1998) "Alcohol and social complexity in ancient Western Asia." *Current Anthropology* 39:3. 297-322
[41] Joffe, 1998
[42] Crawford, H. (1981) "Some fire installations from Abu Salabikh, Iraq." *Paléorient* 7:2. 105-144
[43] Joffe, 1998
[44] Powell, M. A. (1995) "Metrology and Mathematics in Ancient Mesopotamia". In Sasson, J. M. (ed.) *Civilizations of the Ancient Near East*. New York: Charles Scribner's Sons.
[45] Powell, 1995

distribution, and use of these vessels contributed to daily life in Uruk. These standardized vessels were mass-produced through the use of molds, either in the ground or free-standing, and made of wood.[46] Skilled craftsmen could take as little as one minute to make each one, and being so simple in form, they could be manufactured by laborers with no experience in ceramics, and with no tools other than an existing beveled-rim bowl.[47] They were fired in kilns at specialized "activity" sites, such as those found in Ur and Uruk.[48] Their precise function has been heavily disputed by scholars, as to whether they were used as disposable ration vessels for the distribution of raw grain,[49] or as a form of census-taking for the distribution and availability of labor,[50] or as containers for votive offerings. Regardless, beveled-rim bowls were used in Uruk in administrative, religious, and domestic spheres in juxtaposition with storage areas for food. It can be inferred that they were used by an administrative individual or sector to process a measure of a food product at a centralized distribution site in a standardized and durable form in a manner that reproduced the influence of the rising bureaucracy. All told, it was a package of complexity, a model of dietary practice that becomes part of a cultural identity and an idea that was so simple it could spread widely with only the movement of a single vessel.[51]

---

[46] Goulder, G. (2010) "Administrators' bread: an experiment-based re-assessment of the functional and cultural role of the Uruk bevel-rim bowl." *Antiquity* 84. 351-362
[47] Goulder, 2010
[48] Postgate, J.N. (2002) *Artefacts of Complexity: Tracking the Uruk in the Near East.* Warminster, British School of Archaeology in Iraq
[49] Chazan, M., and Lehner, M. (1990) "An Ancient Analogy: Pot Baked Bread in Ancient Egypt and Mesopotamia." *Paléorient* 16:2. 21-35
[50] Pollock, S. (1992) "Bureaucrats and Managers, Peasants and Pastoralists, Imperialists and Traders: Research on the Uruk and Jemdet Nasr Periods in Mesopotamia." *Journal of World Prehistory* 6:3. 297-336
[51] Goulder, 2010

Jon Onomac's picture of a water trough found at Uruk

Some discoveries made by the ancient Sumerians are still used by Iraqis today. For instance, bitumen is used for waterproofing boat hulls and sealing the roofs of houses. There were public, earthenware pots of drinking water on street corners and the water evaporated on the surface of the vessel in the hot, daytime weather, keeping the water within it cool, a Sumerian invention that is still in use five thousand years later in Baghdad.

Cuneiform Writing

It is unclear whether the Sumerians were the earliest people to develop writing, but theirs is the oldest known writing system in Mesopotamia, and their language has no known resemblance with any others. Their formation of a complex society can be found among the vast majority of Mesopotamian cuneiform texts and iconographic seals used to record transactions such as the issuing of rations, collection of imports, and receipt of goods.

With the development of trade, the Sumerians invented the concept of the "contract." In ancient Mesopotamia, this came in the form of carved cylindrical stone seals, finely engraved with a negative bas relief. When a contract was entered into, or goods needed to be identified, the cylinder was rolled in clay, with the mark it left on the clay sealing the transaction. Such seals were also used by priests and nobles of the city on everything from important letters to legal decrees.[52] The act of sealing represented the authorization of a transaction by a recognized official who regulated the places where goods, such as food and drink, were produced, where they were assembled, and where they were distributed. Thus, finds of broken and discarded sealings imply locations of storage and distribution of food products, whereas the presence of unfinished or complete bullae indicate the preparation of goods to be sent elsewhere.[53]

---

[52] Collon, D. (2005) *First Impressions, Cylinder Seals in the Ancient Near East*, London: British Museum Press
[53] Pollock, 1992

Cylinder seals found at Uruk

The second system was the use of the cuneiform script, an alphabet of wedge-shaped characters made by impressing a stick into soft clay. It is unknown whether the clay tablets were sometimes left wet, but the ones that have survived for thousands of years to the present day were baked in an oven, left to dry in the air, or hardened by fire when cities were invaded and burned. The earliest examples of cuneiform discovered were found in the Eanna Precinct. Many other cuneiform texts have been found scattered around the ruins on artefacts or impressed on the walls of buildings.

This was also how the Sumerians began to make laws. Very few legal texts from the Sumerian period have been found, but in the early twentieth century, in the Persian city of Susa (located in present-day Iran), archaeologists discovered the Stone of Hammurabi, king of Babylon. This inscribed stone slab had been seized as a trophy by the Elamites, who went on a number of conquests through Mesopotamia during the twelfth century BCE. Hammurabi had the legal code that bears his name, drawn up in 1694 BCE. This code enshrined all of Sumeria's laws, with two hundred and eighty two articles carved on to the stone.[54] They mostly relate to aspects of everyday life in cities like Uruk: commercial transactions, marriages, and inheritances. The king served as the judge. He would order investigations, oversee great public works, and protect the people from abuse by city officials. Hammurabi's laws show that the Sumerians were precursors in many areas of law existing for millennia afterwards. For example, on the back of the stone, one article warns "an eye for an eye," a principle later repeated in Hammurabi's Code and the Law of Moses.[55]

Trade Routes

The goldsmiths of Uruk mastered the techniques of chiseling and soldering gold, which was used also in cups and ceremonial weapons. Also coming from the East were lapis lazuli and other precious materials, such as turquoise. Mother of pearl and sea shells came from Bahrain. These use of these raw materials shows how prosperous Uruk was, and how involved it was in a thriving trade network with neighboring regions, especially since Mesopotamia itself has no major resources apart from water, mud, scattered bitumen deposits, and minor copper sources along its eastern and northern highlands, which spurred inter-regional interaction. Uruk lacked three important resources in particular: precious metals, stone, and wood.

To build their Garden of Eden in Mesopotamia, the Sumerians roamed the world in search of the commodities they lacked, and archaeologists have managed to trace the origins of some of these materials. To get lapis lazuli, the Sumerians sent their trade caravans three thousand kilometers away to the Badakhshan Mountains, in what is now northern Pakistan and southern Afghanistan. Archaeologists have established this trade in lapis lazuli–which has continued for millennia–began with the Sumerian civilization, opening trade routes crossing over Eurasia, predating the Great Silk Road by more than three thousand years.[56]

The lack of wood in the Mesopotamian desert was a key issue facing the people of Uruk. To get this rare commodity, used almost exclusively as a building material and to create the occasional precious object, the Sumerians ventured to Syria, Anatolia, and the mountains of Lebanon on expeditions lasting several months. Bas reliefs found in southern Mesopotamia show Sumerian loggers chopping down cedars and loading them onto ships before sailing back down the Euphrates.[57] Today, cedar forests are few and far between in the region, because after the

---

[54] Roth, M. T. (1997) *Law Collections from Mesopotamia and Asia Minor*. Atlanta: Scholars Press
[55] Roth, 1997
[56] Herrmann, 1966
[57] Leick, 2001

Sumerians, all ancient civilizations used cedar, gradually cutting down almost all of the forests in antiquity.

Bitumen was acquired from sites like Hit, a small town on the banks of the Euphrates almost five hundred kilometers north of Uruk. Tar and sulphur erupt from the earth there, and archaeologists believe that the Sumerians collected it from the riverbanks as it floated down the Euphrates.[58] The people of Hit, Iraq, still collect tar by methods that remain unchanged for thousands of years. Before taking the tar out of the water they coat their hands in sand so they are able to handle the hot material.[59] The Sumerians used bitumen to waterproof their boats, but its main uses were a sealants for bricks and to waterproof public building foundations, a precaution needed as a result of the annual flooding of the Euphrates.

The Spread of Uruk Culture

The view of a nation as a specific and bounded geopolitical entity is a historically created condition originating in 17th century Europe, concerned with the division of landscape in which identity was absolute, boundaries were fixed, and legal restrictions were enforced. It must be made clear that the ancient Mesopotamian kingdoms and empires did not function in this way.[60] The natural boundaries offered by the rivers, mountains, and deserts of the land were not absolute, but zones of great interaction throughout the millennia.[61] Throughout history, trade caravans, military expeditions, and countless numbers of migrants crossed over these boundaries from neighboring lands, each of which had an influence on Mesopotamian society and culture in its own manner.

Archaeologists view ideas of territoriality and boundaries as a convenient fiction used to map out and analyze polities, built upon an abstraction of landscape. In examining ancient Mesopotamia, the notion of "territory" and state has been presented in different ways, and there exists no definitive consensus about how one can describe ancient Mesopotamian "states" like that of Uruk. Some claim they were organized as territorial entities under public authorities, encompassing many communities in its boundaries with a centralized government, drafted armies, collective labor, and taxation.[62] Others take a broader perspective, maintaining that states can be identified as autonomous political units by their legal systems or by the extent that they use coercion to enforce power over their population.[63] These two perspectives assume that states have more or less known limits, where people believe there is a bounded territory representing the state's jurisdiction and control, and that states have an organizational quality remaining

---

[58] Leick, 2001
[59] Bilkadi, Z. (1984) "Bitumen - A History." *Aramco World*, 35: 6.
[60] Wilkinson, 2000
[61] Bahrani, 1998
[62] Raaflaub, K., and Nathan R, (eds) (1999) *War and Society in the Ancient and Medieval Worlds: Asia, The Mediterranean, Europe, and Mesoamerica*. Cambridge: Center for Hellenic Studies, Harvard University. . .
[63] Trigger, B. G. (2003) *Understanding Early Civilizations: A Comparative Study*. New York: Cambridge University Press. .

constant through time.

However, ancient Mesopotamia was composed of many fragmented (and often overlapping) cultural, linguistic, or ethnic spheres.[64] In this sense, their boundaries were porous, permeable, and flexible. Moreover, they were selectively identified and defended by certain groups, depending on their historic context. What does the nature and structure of Uruk tell us about its relationship with its surroundings as well as with other city-states of contemporary Mesopotamia? Archaeologists have recently tried to look at Uruk beyond the boundaries of the city walls and immediate hinterland, in an attempt to start building a regional understanding of the importance of routes and their dynamics to understand the nature of the communities they connect.

The Uruk expansion occurred during the fifth millennium BCE as northern sites made contact with the south. This is indicated by cones, bullae, and seals traditionally identified with the northern sites, though increasingly used in areas of southern Mesopotamia.[65] The spread of urbanization was the most important process that took place during this period, marking the transition from subsistence farming to the emergence of cities in southern Mesopotamia. Following the model set by Uruk, other cities from this period were defined by factors including the emergence of a bureaucracy with a centralized governing body; social stratification in the form of a military, religious, or political elite; increasing levels of craft and economic specialization; and the emergence of full-time professionals.[66] Furthermore, many cities can be identified by the monumental structures and temples built in the urban landscape, indicating the emergence of organized religion.

---

[64] Smith, A. T. (2003) *The Political Landscape: Constellations of Authority in Early Complex Polities*. Berkeley: University of California Press. .
[65] Bogucki, 1990
[66] Bogucki, 1990

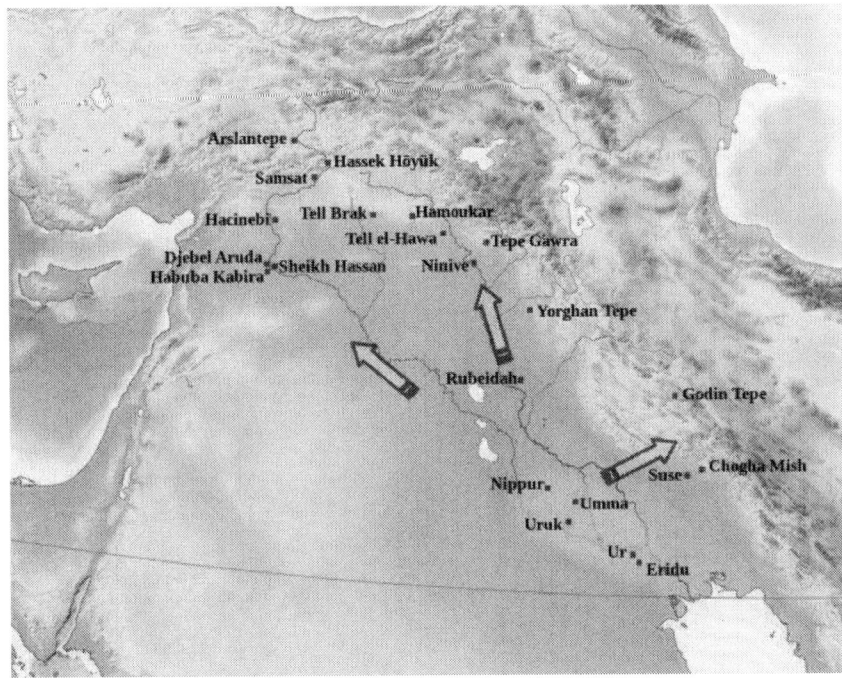

A map demonstrating the spread of the Uruk expansion

Tell Brak (also known as Nagar or Nawar) was a settlement from the seventh millennium BCE that grew to be one of the largest cities in northern Mesopotamia during the fourth millennium before shrinking in size at the beginning of the third millennium.[67] The tell is surrounded by a raised area with hollow ways that were used to direct water from hydraulic catchments in the north, though it is not clear if these hollow ways were intentionally developed to redirect water from catchment areas, or part of the natural drainage net responsible for redirecting runoff from rainfall.[68]

Tell Brak was a religious center from its earliest periods as seen in the famous "Eye Temple" devoted to Belet-Nagar. The temple is decorated with a mosaic of geometric designs made with riemchen.[69] Also at Tell Brak are some of the earliest indications of the spread of a specialized

---

[67] Bryce, T. (2009) *The Routledge Handbook of the Peoples and Places of Ancient Western Asia: The Near East from the Early Bronze Age to the Fall of the Persian Empire*. London: Routledge. .
[68] Wilkinson, T. J. (2007) Ancient Near Eastern Route Systems: From the Ground Up. *Archatlas* (http://www.archatlas.dept.shef.ac.uk/workshop/TWilkinson07.php)
[69] Ristvet, 2014

craft production originating in Uruk and other urban sites in southern Mesopotamia. Instead of each household making its own pottery, there were people whose job it was to do so. One particularly fascinating artifact to come from Tell Brak is a chalice made of obsidian and attached to a marble base, materials that would have had to travel over huge distances to reach the site.[70] The conspicuous consumption of materials such as this would have marked out certain, powerful individuals as being more powerful. At the time when Tell-Brak was becoming an urban site, individuals were beginning to set themselves apart socially and most probably, politically.[71]

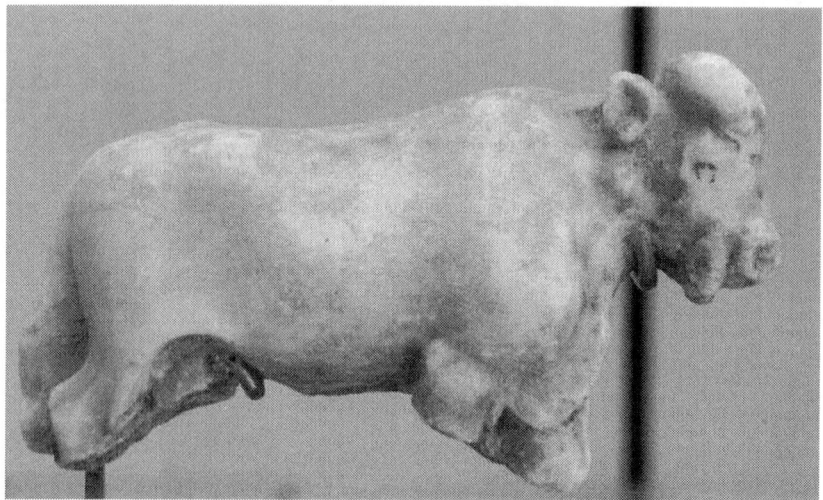

A bull sculpture found in Uruk

---

[70] Bryce, 2009
[71] Ristvet, 2014

The Mask of Warka found at Uruk

The Uruk expansion occurred elsewhere around Mesopotamia and even further afield. In the region of the Upper Euphrates, the religious acropolis of Tell Qannas shows evidence of riemchen bricks and beveled-rim bowls in ancient Anatolia, and riemchen mosaics have been found at Samsat.[72] The architectural styles of structures in Hassek Huyuk also share similarities with those of the southern Mesopotamia.[73] The spread of writing systems is indicated by the seal impressions found at Arslantepe, and beveled-rim bowls were discovered by archaeologists in Tepecik. One of the most important archaeological sites of this period in Anatolia is Çatalhöyük,

---

[72] Bryce, 2009
[73] Bryce, 2009

a city of around one thousand houses, about half of which were approximately twenty five square meters in size, making them suitable to accommodate a large nuclear family,[74] with an estimated total population of around five thousand people. Houses there were plastered, some of which had elaborate wall paintings, wall reliefs, and animal skull shrines, and like the Sumerians, religion seemed to be a driving force in their society.[75]

How did the Uruk culture expand so far during this period? Some archaeologists insist that one way to determine this is through the flow of valuable materials from their source to urban centers. For example, the rich mineral resources on the highland rim of the Fertile Crescent may have been a key factor in the formation of complex trade networks, a periphery waiting for a core.[76] The extraction and long-distance trade of lapis lazuli from Afghanistan, or the exchange of gold, silver, and copper from Eastern Anatolia to lowland Mesopotamia in the fourth millennium BCE, act as indicators of potential catchment areas that urban powers were willing to trade with for luxury materials. Each day, the repetitive exchange of ideas and materials took place along local pathways, whereas macro-scale interactions–involving high-value materials–took place along highways.[77]

This trade can also provide insight into the relationship between sedentary urban communities and their nomadic neighbors, as route-systems led from the top-down, from the desires of lowland urbanizing elites influencing the actions of upland communities.[78] Since many important resources were not found in Mesopotamia, traders at this time had to travel far from their city-states in search of commodities, and interact with nomadic middlemen to acquire certain materials. Some claim that colonies were established in cities across Eurasia by these traveling merchants through which technological designs and ideologies were transmitted.[79] Lapis lazuli discovered in ancient Egypt lends weight to this hypothesis, showing that routes to Afghanistan from the Mediterranean region were in existence at this time. The Uruk culture appears to have expanded as far as ancient Egypt by the Naqada II/Gerzean period (ca. 3500 BCE —3200 BCE), as indicated by the cylinder seals at Tell al Fara in the Nile Delta.[80]

Jemdet Nasr and the Early Dynastic Periods

Sumerian society and culture flourished during the third millennium BCE. In the late Uruk period, many of the northern sites were being abandoned in favor of new settlements being established further south in the vicinity of Uruk, which had doubled in size.[81] This trend

---

[74] Hodder, I. (ed.) (1996) *On the Surface: Çatalhöyük 1993–95*. Cambridge: McDonald Institute for Archaeological Research and British Institute of Archaeology at Ankara. .
[75] Hodder, 1996
[76] Sherratt, A. (2004) "Trade Routes: The Growth of Urban Supply Routes 3500 BC – AD 1500." *Archatlas* (http://www.archatlas.dept.shef.ac.uk/Trade/Trade.php)
[77] Wilkinson, 2007
[78] Wilkinson, 2000
[79] Sundsdal, K. (2011) "The Uruk Expansion: Culture Contact, Ideology and Middlemen." *Norwegian Archaeological Review*, 44: 2. 164 - 185. .
[80] Wilkinson, R. H. (2000) *The Complete Temples of Ancient Egypt*. London: Thames & Hudson

continued in the Jemdet Nasr and Early Dynastic periods, as Uruk's prosperity continued to grow.

The Jemdet Nasr period is identified by the growth of a league of city-states in central-southern Mesopotamia. Political, religious, and mercantile alliances were formed between these states, as indicated by seal impressions found on tablets that bear the symbol of Inanna, god of Uruk. The Early Dynastic period was marked by a dramatic increase of sites and population around Mesopotamia. This was a period of constant petty struggles between neighboring cities, and a time of political fragmentation alongside cultural integration.

Though temples seem to have served as centers of power in the fourth millennium, there was a shift toward more secular leadership by famous male figures in the Early Dynastic period.[82] Cult followings of certain figures grew in the context of intensive political competition. These powerful individuals showed off their superiority and power through "conspicuous consumption": the sourcing of expensive and rare raw materials from other regions, and the acquisition of objects from far-off lands to be brought to the cultural capitals for display, which facilitated trade connections with other regions.

---

[81] Rothman, 2001
[82] Rothman, 2001

An ancient depiction of Innana

Other sites influenced by the Uruk culture flourished during this period, as indicated by burials at the Royal Cemetery of Ur, which show an ostentatious display of luxury material wealth in line with the conspicuous consumption of living leaders. This conspicuous consumption was not restricted to objects and materials, but also people, with respect to evidence of human sacrifice.

In one tomb, a royal figure called Lady Puabi was interred with numerous handmaidens and buried with a splendid array of rare and expensive objects, including the so-called "Queen's Lyre," designed in the form of a bull, of which only the head and fragments of the body have survived to this day.[83] The bull's head on this lyre has eyes of lapis lazuli set into a gold face. The harp itself was decorated with shells and precious stones. For their final journey with the queen, the sacrificed servants each wore a spectacular diadem of gold bands and precious stones, and their brows were embellished with a braiding of beech leaves made of thin beaten leaf from which rose three flowers of gold.[84] Lady Puabi was also buried with a magnificent headdress made of gold, silver, lapis lazuli, copper, and carnelian in the form of a ram peering through a thicket.[85]

Trade became increasingly important in the context of conspicuous consumption, corresponding with the expansion of sedentary sites from southern Mesopotamia into its marginal zones. The site of Al-Rawda was occupied during the second half of the third millennium BCE, where geomatic surveys have revealed a dense infrastructure of buildings organized into a network of concentric and radial streets, all set within a fortified enclosure.[86] Al-Rawda's relationship with wider Mesopotamia is indicated by five massive gateways in the city's walls, and the routes leading to and from the city.

The monumentality of these entrances and the excavated exotic items found in the main temple to which the main roads lead, indicates the city's involvement with the Early Bronze Age trade routes from Western Syria to the Euphrates Valley.[87] Finds including shells from the Mediterranean Sea and the Arabo-Persian Gulf, agate from India, lapis lazuli from Badakhshan, and possibly Egyptian alabaster, indicate that Al-Rawda was taking an active part in this trade route, as a peripheral location strategically placed by its core and planned to exploit long-distance trade networks. Other towns with similar infrastructural designs were established during this time, such as Mari in the Euphrates River valley, and Tell Chuera in Northern Syria.[88] One suggested role for such a regular, organized, urban environment in a marginal location such as this may be as a gateway community for communication with pastoralists and the exploitation of local resources.

---

[83] de Schauensee, M. (2002) *Two Lyres from Ur*. Philadelphia: University of Philadelphia Museum of Archaeology and Anthropology
[84] de Schauensee, 2002
[85] Baadsgaard, A., Monge, J., Cox, S., and Zettler, R. L. (2012) "Bludgeoned, Burned, and Beautified: Reevaluating Mortuary Practices in the Royal Cemetery of Ur." in *Sacred killing: the archaeology of sacrifice in the ancient Near East*. Winona Lake.: Eisenbrauns. 125 - 158. .
[86] Castel and Peltenburg, 2006
[87] Wilkinson, T. J. (2000b) "Settlement and Land Use in the Zone of Uncertainty in Upper Mesopotamia." In R.M. Jas (ed.) *Rainfall and agriculture in Northern Mesopotamia: Proceedings of the Third MOS Symposium*. Leiden: Nederlands Instituut voor het Nabije Oosten. 3 - 35. .
[88] Castel and Peltenburg, 2006

The Fall of Uruk

Following the period of political fragmentation marked by the Early Dynastic period came two hundred years of regional integration. It is believed that the first king to truly unite Sumer was Lugalzagesi of Umma (2360 – 2336 BCE), who also became its last.[89] He is said to have conquered all the other Sumerian city-states and then subjugated the rest of Mesopotamia and Syria, but after decades on the throne, he was overthrown by Sargon of Akkad (r. ca. 2340 – 2284 CE). Sargon created the world's first empire, stretching the length and breadth of the Fertile Crescent.

Texts such as the red limestone Victory Stele of Naram-Sin (ca. 2254 – 2218 BCE) provide invaluable insight into the events of this period.[90] This stela was set up far away from Mesopotamia, in the Iranian site of Susa. It depicts the victory of Naram-Sin, grandson of Sargon, over the mountainous Lullubi people in the distinctive landscape of the Zagros Mountains. Kingship was believed to have been handed down from the gods, and could be transferred from one city to another. By portraying this victory, in marching over the steep slopes of enemy territory to crush his opponents, Naram-Sin reaches the same elevated position as the gods and reflects the hegemony of the Akkadians in the early third millennium.

---

[89] Crawford, 2004
[90] Crawford, 2004

A sculpture of Lugal-kisal-si, king of Uruk

A mask believed to depict Sargon

Naram-Sin's victory stela

However, Sargon's empire quickly fell to insurrection and invasion by the hordes of the Guti, a nomadic people from the Zagros Mountains, who ruled in the south for a century or so. Eventually, they too were thrown out in an uprising which inaugurated the Third Dynasty of Ur. This dynasty was established by the king Ur Nammu, and under his rule, Sumerian culture and civilization once again prospered.[91] There was peace throughout the land, the legal system was strengthened, agriculture prospered, and towns and temples were rebuilt. However, after a century the nomadic Amorites–also known as the Semites–shattered the Ur III Empire, and the Sumerian language was gradually replaced.[92]

The next few centuries were turbulent, as several city-states vied for supremacy in southern Mesopotamia. Then, in 1750 BCE, the people of Uruk and the other city-states became part of

---

[91] Bryce, 2009
[92] Crawford, 2004

the politically unified empire of Babylonia, founded by King Hammurabi. Hammurabi's empire–which included Mesopotamia, Syria, and part of Anatolia–was a powerful one.[93] After consolidating his rule over the warring city-states, Hammurabi wrote the first of his law codes. The empire retained its power for more than three hundred years.

By around 1400 BCE, another people–the Assyrians–emerged as a dominant force in the region, centering around the city of Assur. The Assyrians had one major advantage over the powerful Babylonian empire–the horse–which they used to devastate the Babylonian armies so accustomed to fighting on foot. Babylon fell to these conquerors, who gained control over most of Mesopotamia.

Under these successive powers, many transformations took place in the city of Uruk, though it would be incorrect to say the earlier Sumerian culture was simply "replaced" by those of the Akkadians and Babylonians. Instead, it should be seen as an innovative hybrid between what already existed in the city and that which came from outside of the Sumerian cultural sphere. For example, in the third century BCE, the Reš Temple Precinct–also known as the Kullaba Precinct–was added to the center of Uruk, west of the earlier Eanna Precinct. The *bīt*, as this style of temple was known, was a stage building of Akkadian origins made popular by the Babylonians, and likely housed political performances whilst playing a parallel role as a temple.[94] Although a new construction, the Reš Temple of Uruk was built in a manner that resembled the temple precincts of the earlier periods of the city, emphasizing the continuous relevance of these sites for the city population.

A second, vast, temple complex was built in this time as well–the Akītu Temple–where Babylonian priests performed ceremonies dedicated to Anu each spring.[95] The Irigal Temple was a square complex constructed south of the Reš Temple in approximately 200 BCE, used as the house of worship for the god Ishtar and Nana.[96]

Gilgamesh is believed by most scholars to have been a real historical figure, the fifth king of Uruk, who existed during the third millennium BCE.[97] Yet his life is steeped in a myth that, in many ways, reflects the rise and fall of Uruk and the Sumerian culture. He was the Sumerians' hero, and the stories of his adventures were famous throughout Mesopotamia, summing up the history of the rise and fall of the Sumerian civilization at that time.

Gilgamesh was a just king and a great builder who also challenged the gods. He tamed savage

---

[93] Bryce, 2009
[94] Ristvet, L. (2014b) "Between ritual and theatre: political performance in Seleucid Babylonia." *World Archaeology*, 46:2. 256-269
[95] Downey, S. B. (1988) *Mesopotamian Religious Architecture: Alexander Through the Parthians*. Princeton: Princeton University Press
[96] Potts, D.T. (1997) *Mesopotamian Civilization: The Material Foundations*. New York: Cornell University Press
[97] George, A. (2003) *The Babylonian Gilgamesh Epic - Introduction, Critical Edition and Cuneiform Texts*. Oxford: Oxford University Press. .

tribes and went to the distant Cedar Forest–considered the home of the gods–to confront Humbaba, the fire-eating monster. During their fight, Gilgamesh cut off the monster's head, and returned with it to Uruk in triumph. To punish him, the goddess Inanna sent a celestial bull to destroy the city. The bull dried up the meadows and rivers of the land, and opened up deep crevices into which people fell to their deaths.

The sudden fall of ancient Near Eastern empires is not unprecedented. Kingdoms, dynasties, and empires all eventually fall, and the people of the Near East must have been mentally accustomed to the concept of the structures and foundations in their way of life collapsing. After ruling Mesopotamia for three thousand years, the Sumerian civilization, attacked from all sides, collapsed. The pomp of their cities was over, and so was their influence over the land. Irrigation canals at Uruk gradually dried up, walls of houses and temples collapsed under the combined assault of the sun, rain, and wind, and the clay of the bricks turned to dust, leaving only a shapeless mass above the dunes as the last vestige of a civilization's grandeur.

It's still an open question as to how the Sumerians completely disappeared. Conspicuous consumption and the acquisition of resources could have caused the eventual decline. In approximately 1200 BCE, mankind discovered iron as an asset–it was easier to work, stronger, and had more applications than the copper that the Sumerians had previously used. The problem was that Mesopotamia had little iron ore of its own, and they had to stretch their trade routes farther away to obtain the precious material. Of course, they could not compete with regions that had easier access to the iron ore, and it was these people that eventually played a much larger role in the region.

Climate probably played the largest role in the decline and fall of Uruk. Despite their inventive abilities, the farmers and rulers were powerless to keep their resources from dwindling. The irrigation system made the people of Uruk powerful, but it also contributed to their destruction. Uruk was originally built on the southwest shore of the Euphrates, but the river moved over time, and today, the ruined city is located a far distance northeast of the river. The mud-brick buildings of the city would not have endured against the floods caused by the encroaching river. Furthermore, the satellite settlements and farms surrounding the city, which supplied the population with grain, experienced further problems as a result of the desertification of the land.

As three thousand years of irrigation water evaporated, the salt buried deep in the land rose to the surface. In the end, the fields surrounding Uruk were covered in a white crust of salt, baked hard by the sun. Wheat could no longer grow in the sterile soil. Local people are still plagued by this problem today–in some areas, the earth resembles a cracked, uncultivated, desert, despite the fact that this area was once known as the Fertile Crescent.

Faced with climate change and desertification, the farmers could find no solution, and the weakened city was unable to face economic competition from large cities elsewhere in Mesopotamia. By the 8th century BCE, Uruk was finished. The Babylonians fell to the Assyrians around the same time, and although the Babylonians would eventually manage to regain their independence from Assyria in the 7th century, they had no use for the sterile land of southern Mesopotamia. Beneath the pitiless sun, the city of Uruk returned to the dust.

Archaeological Work

In the 1850s, when archaeologists first went to Iraq, they went in search of the region's Biblical past. In the mid-19th century, all that was known of ancient Mesopotamia was what could be read in the Old Testament. French and British archaeologists competed to discover what they could of these semi-mythological lands, focusing their interest on the site of Babylon and instead finding the remains of much older civilizations. They uncovered an unsuspected civilization, buried beneath the sands, but what was so special about what they found, and why did a civilization develop in that part of the world at all? These were the questions asked by Mesopotamia's earliest researchers.

The first archaeologists to see the ruins of Uruk must have been speechless, because before them lay a confusing landscape of narrow streets, squares, and the remains of houses, granaries, and temples. Today, the land around Uruk is an arid desert, several kilometers away from the present day course of the nearest rivers, making it difficult to picture it as a once-thriving city in which its inhabitants lived off the land. When they found the ruins of Sumerian dams on this barren land, the archaeologists of the 19th century faced an enigma in attempting to figure out how people could have lived in this desert, so far from a source of fresh water.

Eventually, it was learned that Uruk evolved into a vastly different landscape from that which exists today. Two hundred and fifty kilometers south of Baghdad and one hundred and sixty kilometers north of Uruk is the desert city of Nippur, its ruined temple rising above the sandy dunes. It was during excavation of this site that archaeologists first discovered the extent to which the ancient landscape had changed over time. There, they found a clay tablet depicting a map of Nippur, with the exact locations of the temple, the city wall, and the Euphrates River, including a channel where it had been diverted to supply the city with water.[98] The city had, therefore, been built beside the water, but changes in landform and the sheer force of the annual flooding had changed the course of the river over time.

The earliest excavations to take place at Uruk were done under William Loftus, a British explorer, between 1850 and 1854. More intensive excavations took place in the early 1910s by the German Oriental Society, led by Julius Jordan. It was during this season that the Reš Temple was discovered, as well as the walls of Gilgamesh. The German archaeologists returned to southern Iraq on many more occasions before and after World War II, but by using trenching, an excavation technique typical of this early period in archaeology, they caused much damage to the site and ignored much of the valuable information that could have been supplied through the

---

[98] McCown, D. E. (1952) "Excavations at Nippur, 1948–50." *Journal of Near Eastern Studies*, 11:3. 169 – 176. .

careful study of the stratigraphic relationships of the tell's many layers. The modern methodologies of the German Archaeological Institute, which has undertaken excavation at Uruk since the beginning of the 21st century, have been much less damaging and more informative. Using geophysical surveys alongside limited excavations, it is mainly from these projects that most of what is known of the city itself has been revealed.[99]

Loftus

Unique artifacts offer a very small, detailed source of information. Luckily for the archaeologists, the people of Mesopotamia did not have regularly scheduled times or places to get rid of their household waste. It was, instead, simply dumped on the streets of the city, leaving

---

[99] van Ess, M. and Fassbinder, J. (2005) "Magnetic prospection of Uruk (Warka) Iraq." *La Prospection Géophysique: Dossiers d'Archeologie*, 308. 20–25

enormous amounts of material remains for archaeologists to excavate and study very near the locations they were used. The surface distribution of pottery was analyzed to indicate where people may have lived in the past. There is also a wealth of textual sources offering unique historical perspectives of contemporary life in Uruk. Like the ceramic remains, these are usually located in the cities from which they originated, as invading conquerors preferred to carry away valuable gold or silver objects instead. Cuneiform was used by many languages and when fired, the tablets it was written on are well preserved. Inscriptions and writing on perishable materials may have also existed, but they did not survive.

Over time, archaeological attention in the region was turned away from its traditional focus on temporal components to the detailed analyses of stratigraphic relationships to reveal chronological sequences of events in a small area. Surveying, both intensive and extensive, became the dominant methodology used to investigate the entire region. By considering the horizontal, spatial components of the landscape, archaeologists could get a new and exciting view of the past. Whereas aerial photographs have proved to be of limited use in the Near East, having never been done in a systematic manner, archaeologists have, over the past decades, made use of satellite imagery, such as the declassified CORONA satellite images and recent Quickbird software. CORONA images and excavations have proven to be very effective in the study of ancient trade routes, in particular. Despite being too dated to be used for intelligence purposes, they provide archaeologists with images taken in a systematic manner through the 1960s and 1970s, effectively making a preservation-by-record of the landscape at the time.[100] This is of particular value due to the effects of modernization and development in the region, as the present landscape has been altered dramatically due to the expansion of towns and intensive mechanical agriculture, shown, for example, at Tell Brak in the Khabur Basin area.[101]

The discovery of the Mesopotamian civilization was exceptional because it allowed scholars to gradually realize that an extremely diverse and highly developed, complex society once existed in a world they were not aware of apart from what was described in the Bible. Many people believed that civilization began with the Greeks, but what archaeologists discovered in the sands of Iraq was evidence that something once existed long before them, influencing the development of classical civilization.

Several contemporary texts refer to the Sumerian temperament. Experiencing so many of the hazards of nature, it is no wonder they are described as conscious of the brevity and fragility of life. The building works they engaged in and bas reliefs they left behind (some images show men relaxing and/or drinking beer from large vessels through straws), indicate the enormous achievement of a people living in a terribly hostile environment, inspiring their most beautiful

---

[100] Ur, J. (2003) "CORONA Satellite Photography and Ancient Road Networks: A Northern Mesopotamian Case Study." *Antiquity* 77: 102-115
[101] Ur, J. (2007)" Agricultural and Pastoral Landscapes in the Near East: Case Studies using CORONA Satellite Photography." *ArchAtlas (*http://www.archatlas.dept.shef.ac.uk/workshop/Ur07.php)

myths.

It's their story that the Bible tells. Like the builders of the Tower of Babel, the men and women of Uruk were eventually scattered across the land. The water the city had both feared and relied upon brought about its own destruction. Having controlled the floods of the Euphrates for thousands of years, the people of Uruk were eventually swept away by history.

For a very long time, little was known of life in Uruk, but in the arid desert surrounding the site, traces of the ancient past can be found. Can one truly speak of the decline, let alone the disappearance, of a civilization? In many ways, to talk of the "decline" of the Sumerians is an incorrect use of the word. Theirs was a civilization reaching its peak after producing many wonderful things and great individuals, and their inventions, philosophies, and stories never vanished. Instead, their culture has been transmitted through the ages, first across Anatolia via the Greeks and Persians, and then across the Mediterranean world as a whole. All the while, the classical world inherited the achievements of the Mesopotamian civilization without realizing its source. In the end, the people of Uruk left mankind with the legacy of their wealth, traces of their creative genius, and a sense of the extraordinary fragility of civilizations.

Ur

Chapter 1: An Inspiration for Mesopotamia

An arch located in Ur

The Old Testament is full of many stories about biblical peoples who modern archaeologists and biblical scholars have verified as factual and can be beneficial to understanding other peoples and places in the ancient Near East such as Ur. In the book of Genesis the patriarch Abraham and his family are described as having lived in Ur. The book reads: "Now these are the generations of Terah: Terah begat Abram, Nahor, and Haran; and Haran begat Lot. And Haran died before his father Terah in the land of his nativity, in Ur of the Chaldees. And Abram and Nahor took wives: the name of Abram's wife was Sarai; and the name of Nahor's wife, Milcah, the daughter of Haran, the father of Milcah, and the father of Iscah. But Sarai was barren; she had no child. And Terah took Abram his son, and Lot the son of Haran his son's, and Sarai his daughter in law, his son Abram's wife; and they went forth with them from Ur of the Chaldees, to go into the land of Canaan; and they came unto Harran, and dwelt there." (Gen. 11:27-31)

This passage relates some interesting and important aspects of Ur as it pertains to both its significance among non-Sumerian peoples and its location in the ancient Near East. It is interesting that although Abraham and his family were not Sumerians, Ur is listed in the biblical account as their first home. Many cities in the ancient Near East had quarters that were designated for foreigners: Memphis, Egypt had a Greek quarter in its later history and Alexandria, Egypt was divided into ethnic neighborhoods, so the idea of ethnically diverse cities was not an alien concept in the ancient Near East. In the case of Ur, it was probably a center for non-Sumerian pastoral peoples who had camps near the city gates (Kitchen 2003, 316). Kitchen also explains that although other cities named Ur existed, the "Ur of the Chaldees" of the Bible was clearly a reference to the Sumerian city (Kitchen 2003, 316). The Chaldeans were a people who lived in southern Mesopotamia who would later conquer most of Babylon, including the kingdom of Israel, during the seventh and sixth centuries BCE, so although the reference was culturally and chronologically incorrect, it was geographically close.

In terms of modern geographical references, Ur was located about halfway between the modern city of Baghdad and the head of the Persian Gulf in what is now the modern nation-state of Iraq (Woolley 1982, 12). Ur was a key city in the wider geographic region known as the "Fertile Crescent," which encompassed the Levant and Mesopotamia. The region of Mesopotamia, so named by the Greeks as it meant "the land between the two rivers", is a large region that today is comprised of the modern nation-states of Iraq and part of Syria and sits between the Tigris and Euphrates rivers. Mesopotamia was further sub-divided into more regions in ancient times: Assyria was in the far north, Babylonia and Akkad were in the middle, and Sumer, which is where Ur was located, was in the far south. Ur was located a few miles south of the Euphrates River (Van de Mieroop 2007, 46), but was connected to the river and the rest of the region through canals that were first built as early as 6,000 BCE (Van de Mieroop 2007, 13). The especially fertile region produced enough food to feed a large population, but it lacked many other resources needed to build large monuments.

The rich alluvial soil of Mesopotamia helped produce copious amounts of grain for its inhabitants, but offered little else in terms of timber, stone, or other precious commodities such as gold, silver, and lapis lazuli (Kuhrt 2010, 1:21). The absence of these materials may not appear to be a problem in terms of building a basic society, but for a society to attain the next level of development and become a true civilization, monuments are considered vital by most modern anthropologists and historians. By the early third millennium BCE, the Sumerians developed complex trade networks that linked most of the ancient Near East and brought rare goods into their cities such as Uruk and Ur (Van de Mieroop 2007, 35). Despite the influx of rare items into Ur, the Sumerians preferred to build most of their major monuments from the readily available mud brick instead of stone (Frankfort 1996, 18). Mud brick is an relatively easy material to work with and capable of producing large monuments, but as Ur's most impressive monument, the Ziggurat of Ur, will attest, it does not stand the test of time as well as stone monuments. Since most of Ur's great monuments have not weathered the ages very well, its modern discovery was an incredible event in itself.

Chapter 2: The Modern Discovery of Ur

Pictures of excavation work at Ur

The discovery of Ur in the modern period followed much the same pattern that took place when other ancient cultures and cities were rediscovered. The period known as the Enlightenment in the eighteenth century was a period when Western Europeans began to question the legitimacy of monarchal government, organized religion, and life itself. Philosophers such as Brit John Locke and Frenchman Jean-Jacques Rousseau wrote books that questioned the nature of government and influenced the revolutions in America and France. The Enlightenment also raised ideas such as popular education and questioned standard ideas of history. Before the Enlightenment, most Europeans viewed the cultures of the Old Testament as the only people worthy of study before Hellenic civilization, but the attention given to those peoples was cursory at best. Enlightenment scholars began to view the past more critically and believed that there was more to the ancient world than the Greeks, Romans, and the biblical peoples. A recent scholar of the Enlightenment summarized the new attitude: "Eighteenth-century concerns focused on three major areas: the debate generated by the idea of a "universal" human nature; the associated debate on the meaning of human history; and the debate generated over the worth and nature of civilization." (Outram 1995, 65).

Although few significant discoveries concerning the ancient Near East were made during the eighteenth century, the groundwork was laid for monumental archaeological and historiographical advances to be made during the nineteenth century.

The nineteenth century witnessed the decipherment of the ancient Egyptian hieroglyphic script through the translation of the Rosetta Stone and a plethora of other finds throughout the Near East. The kingdoms of the Assyrians and Hittites were rediscovered and the lost city of Ur was found buried under a mound of dirt and rubble. In 1853 British archaeologist J.E. Taylor was traversing Iraq, looking for ancient Mesopotamian ruins and artefacts for the British Museum, when he came across a large mound near the Euphrates River. After some investigation, Taylor excavated the mound and soon learned that he had discovered the lost city of Ur, the "Ur of the Chaldees" mentioned in Genesis (Woolley 1982, 12). Taylor's discovery cleared the way for other British archaeologists to make early important finds at Ur; for instance, W.K. Loftus unearthed a mosaic covered wall and numerous other smaller artifacts were discovered there during the nineteenth century (Woolley 1982, 37). The most important archaeological work done at Ur was conducted by Englishman Leonard Woolley, who began excavations of the city in 1922 and completed his work of the necropolis, which will be discussed extensively below, in 1929 (Woolley 1982, 24). Woolley introduced modern archaeological techniques that are still used today in his work at Ur and advocated a hypothesis that the biblical flood and the one described in the *Epic of Gilgamesh* were one and the same (Woolley 1982, 32). It should be stated that Woolley's flood theory was that it was a localized phenomenon and that the way it is portrayed in both *Gilgamesh* and the Old Testament "is an unreal extension of a very real natural hazard in Sumer" (Woolley 1982, 34). Woolley's localized flood theory has been at least partially confirmed by modern studies that prove the coastline of the Persian Gulf was once considerably further inland at about the site of Ur (Pollock 1999, 30).

Alma Guiness' picture of a mural found at Ur

A war standard found at Ur

Chapter 3: Ur and the Early Dynastic Period (ca. 2900-2500 BCE)

As stated above, Ur's early history was inexorably intertwined with that of the Sumerians, but as the Sumerians consolidated their power in southern Mesopotamia, they dedicated most of their energies to building the city of Uruk, north of Ur. Uruk became the cultural capital of the Sumerians at this early stage as the first writing and the earliest forms of Sumerian art were developed in the city (Kuhrt 2010, 1:23). Excavations of Ur demonstrate that although the city was in existence during the Early Dynastic Period, little of importance in terms of monuments was produced before 2500 BCE, which is not to say the city was of no importance. Around 280 tablets have been excavated at Ur that were dated to approximately 2800 BCE (Van de Mieroop 2007, 42) and studies of these texts have revealed that the city was a religious center from an early time. According to ancient Mesopotamian religious beliefs, each city was the abode of a specific god (Van de Mieroop 2007, 45). Ur was the home of the divine dyad, Nanna and Ningal, who would later become important Mesopotamian deities in other cities during later periods. In fact, it appears that Ur's slow but steady rise to prominence can be linked directly to the importance of Nanna and Ningal. Although there has been a dearth of archaeological evidence excavated at Ur that can be definitively dated to the Early Dynastic Period, the remains of a number of religious buildings have been discovered (Woolley 1982, 46). The existence of these buildings indicates that Ur's significance as a cult center for Nanna and Ningal began quite early as will be discussed more thoroughly below, and the city continued to be an important center for that for over 2,000 years and under the rule of several different dynasties.

Another example of Ur's religious importance during the Early Dynastic Period is evidenced by the large necropolis that Woolley first uncovered during his excavations of the city. Woolley dated the origins of Ur's necropolis to the Early Dynastic Period, which included the tombs of a number of identified nobles (Woolley 1982, 51). The existence of the large Ur necropolis raises important questions about ancient Mesopotamian religion that will be explored more below and it also demonstrates that although Ur may not have been as politically important as Uruk in this early period, the Sumerians attached a special religious and spiritual significance to the city. As Ur continued its slow but steady ascent under the Sumerians during the Early Dynastic Period, the region was suddenly thrust into turmoil when a new dynasty from the region of Akkad to the north of Sumer came to power.

Uruk and the Sumerians' power was challenged by a new Semitic speaking group of people known as the Akkadians, who were led by a vigorous king named Sargon (2340-2284 BCE). Although Sargon and the Akkadians established their language as the *lingua franca* of Mesopotamia and later for diplomacy throughout the entire Near East (Kuhrt 2010, 1:46), they maintained Sumerian cultural continuity throughout the region for the most part, which included patronizing the important temples of Ur. In particular, Sargon installed his daughter as the high priestess, or *entu*, of the moon god Nanna at Ur (Van de Mieroop 2007, 66), which once more demonstrates the continuing religious importance of the city. Subsequent Akkadian rulers also installed their daughters as the high priestesses of Nanna at Ur, which proved to be as politically motivated as it was religious (Van de Mieroop 2007, 66). The Akkadians, who were technically outsiders among the Sumerians, realized that in order for them to be accepted as legitimate rulers they had to patronize the cults of important Sumerian cities such as Ur.

The Akkadians were successful for a considerable period in their efforts to incorporate all of southern Mesopotamia under their rule, but their dynasty was eventually toppled, at least partially by a barbarian horde known as the Gutians (Kuhrt 2010, 1:56-57). The Gutian physical presence in southern Mesopotamia proved to be ephemeral, although texts from the later Third Dynasty of Ur attributed their reign of terror to the angry god Enlil, who the Sumerians believed was ignored by the Akkadians (Kuhrt 2010, 1:57). After the Akkadian dynasty collapsed and the Gutians retreated to their mountain homeland in the east, the political situation in southern Mesopotamia reverted to what it was before the Akkadians came to power, a de-centralized patchwork of competing city-states. The situation would not last long though and after a new order was established, Ur found itself at the height of its power.

Chapter 4: Ur during the Third Dynasty of Ur (2112-2004 BCE)

A tablet dating to the Third Dynasty

The Third Dynasty of Ur, known by modern scholars as Ur III, was a period when Ur became the focal point of Mesopotamian history and its leaders brought back the use of Sumerian in administrative and religious texts (Kuhrt 2010, 1:58-59). It was during the Ur III Dynasty where

The Epic of Gilgamesh was probably first put into writing (Sandars 1972, 8), but most importantly the extant texts from the period paint a fairly clear picture of the composition of the state and the manpower needed to keep it going. For instance, a number of Ur III texts detail the immense amount of manpower needed for building projects, such as for ziggurats and irrigation canals. The irrigation canals were particularly intricate and the farming plots they fed were specifically delineated and appropriated; the leaders of Ur initiated a three-field crop rotation strategy whereby fields were sowed, harvested, and left fallow in a cyclical pattern (Kuhrt 2010, 1:60).

It was also during the Ur III Dynasty that Ur became an important trading center and eventually eclipsed Uruk. Texts indicate that Ur was one of the most important textile centers in Mesopotamia during this period; women and children worked in shops that produced wool and linen clothing and blankets, which were then exported throughout the Near East (Kuhrt 2010, 1:60). Metal production also became an important industry in Ur during the Ur III Dynasty, which the rulers of the city exported, as they did with the textiles, and also used the material to fashion weapons. Cuneiform tablets from the Ur III period demonstrate that all economic activity at Ur has highly centralized, but that trade caravans were carried out by independent merchants (Kuhrt 2010, 1:61). The centralized nature of Ur's economy is best seen in the standardized system of weights and measures used during Ur III. Modern scholars argue that the nature of Ur III's centralized economy would not work well as a straight barter system. Bartering was probably used for small, personal transactions, but for larger transactions that were state sanctioned, some sort of standard must have been used. Metal coils made from gold, silver, bronze, and copper, discovered at Ur are believed by many modern scholars to have been used as a type of standardized weight and proto-currency (Kuhrt 2010, 1:61). If true, then Ur's proto-currency predates the coins used by the Persians by over 1,500 years. The tablets that relate agricultural and economic activity at Ur are truly illuminating, but the same texts also provide much information about the composition of the Ur III state.

The extant administrative documents from the Ur III Dynasty were incredibly well organized and complex, and very similar to the contemporary state of the Old Kingdom of Egypt. Like Egypt, the Ur III state was divided into a number of provinces that were overseen by governors known by the Sumerian word, *ensi*. Each *ensi* was probably culled from the local elite or nobility (Kuhrt 2010, 1:61), which meant that the kings in Ur could dedicate their time and resources to matters such as diplomacy and trade rather than spending time visiting outlying provinces. For the most part the system worked well, probably at least partially due to the fact that the administration of the *ensi* was paralleled by a military one. Each province had at least one general and some, such as the province of Umma, had several generals and only one *ensi* (Van de Mieroop 2007, 77). The generals were never natives of the regions they served in and though often of non-Sumerian ethnic groups, the generals always remained loyal to Ur (van de Mieroop 2007, 77). If an *ensi* had the nerve to rebel against Ur, he first had to contend with the general, or generals, who were serving in his province. The administrative texts show that although the *ensi* and generals were vital to the Ur III state, the most important office under the king was that of the *sukkalmah*.

The *sukkalmah* can best be described as a royal chancellor or viceroy who represented the interests of the Ur III state outside the confines of Ur (Van de Mieroop 2007, 79). He ordered the generals to collect tribute from the provinces and set the number that each locale had to pay (Van de Mieroop 2007, 79). The *sukkalmah* was also responsible for overseeing and administering the marshlands of the Ur III state where there were no true provinces and a lack of law and order persisted (Kuhrt 2010, 1:61). The sources also show that although Ur was the capital of the dynasty, other Sumerian cities, such as Uruk, Nippur, and Eridu, continued to play important roles, especially in religious and ceremonial contexts (Kuhrt 2010, 1:64).

The art of diplomacy was also employed on a sophisticated level by the leaders of the Ur III state. Although the kings of Ur III did not keep any records of treaties or official correspondence texts with other states, or at least none have survived or been discovered, a number of the administrative texts described above also concern diplomacy, which can help paint a picture of how the Ur kings used diplomacy in their affairs. From the texts, it appears that the kings of Ur III scheduled their diplomatic events to coincide with religious festivals and that man who organized any and all diplomatic meetings was the *sukkalmah* (Sharlach 2005, 17-18). The *sukkalmah*, who in this capacity operated similarly to the modern Secretary of State, helped organize the itineraries of the foreign diplomats and emissaries who wished to see the Ur kings. Each festival was a renewal of the king's divine right to rule the Ur state so it would have been important for foreign dignitaries to attend these events (Sharlach 2005, 22).

Chapter 5: Other Monuments and Events at Ur during the Ur III Dynasty

The administrative advances made at Ur during the Ur III Dynasty were very impressive, but a number of other incredible monuments were built in the city during the same period. Since Ur was the capital of the dynasty and the center of Mesopotamian culture during the late third millennium BCE, evidence of these edifices survived into the modern period. Among the most impressive of all the monuments from the Ur III period that survived until modern times was the Ziggurat of Ur.

The Ziggurat of Ur represented the middle point in a long tradition of Mesopotamian religious monument building. Essentially, a ziggurat was a tower that was part of a city's temple complex and was believed to represent a mountain, which was thought to be the earthly abode of whichever god or goddess the temple complex was dedicated (Frankfort 1996, 20-21). As stated above, ziggurats were made primarily of mudbrick, which meant that unfortunately most have not stood the test of time. Ziggurats were first built by the Sumerians, but subsequent rulers of Mesopotamia, including the Babylonians, Elamites, Assyrians, and Neo-Babylonians all built them. In fact, the best preserved ziggurat was built by the Elamite king Untash-Napirisha (ca. 1340-1300 BCE) near the ancient Iranian city of Susa. Untash-Napirisha's ziggurat was built with millions of mudbricks. The bricks of the inner core were sun-dried, while the outer bricks were backed, which no doubt took a considerable amount of fuel (Van de Mieroop 2007, 186). The Ziggurat of Ur was built with the same materials and probably most of the same construction methods as Untash-Napirisha's ziggurat, only nearly 1,000 years earlier, which makes the fact that most of it still stands that much more impressive.

A picture of stamped mudbrick found at Ur

The Ziggurat of Ur was built by the first king of the Ur III Dynasty, Ur-Nammu (ca. 2112-2095 BCE) for the Sumerian moon god and Ur's primary deity, Nanna (Kuhrt 2010, 1:64). Today, only the bottom level of the ziggurat is extant, but based on the structure of other known ziggurats, it would have had three levels and required an immense amount of labor (Kuhrt 2010,

1:64), possibly on the level of that used to construct the Great Pyramids of Giza. The Ziggurat of Ur and all ziggurats for that matter, while vaguely resembling a pyramid, functioned in quite a different manner. Ziggurats, as mentioned above, were part of Mesopotamian temples, while Egyptian pyramids functioned as tombs.

Pictures of the ziggurat's main stairway

The Ziggurat of Ur is the most visibly impressive achievement that was created at Ur, but a number of other important things took place in the city that need to be considered. Ur-Nammu's ambition towards building was only equaled by his desire to expand Ur's dominance, which ultimately led to his death on the battlefield (Kuhrt 2010, 1:63). Ur-Nammu was succeeded by Shulgi (ca. 2094-2047), who completed the Ziggurat of Ur and wrote one of the world's first law codes (Kuhrt 2010, 1:64). The rulers of the Ur III Dynasty lived important and ambitious lives as they expanded the influence of their city, developed a complex bureaucracy, and built great monuments, but archaeological studies by Woolley and later scholars have revealed important information about religion at Ur from how those leaders died.

One of the most intriguing and important archaeological discoveries from Ur is its extensive necropolis. The presence of a necropolis, or a collection of burial tombs, in an ancient Near Eastern archaeological site is not rare – numerous necropolises have been unearthed in Egypt and the tombs of the Achaemenid Persian rulers have been discovered and studied, but what makes the necropolis at Ur important is that it gives modern scholars a window into Mesopotamian ideas of the afterlife that are otherwise unknown. In fact, the necropolis of Ur has no equivalent anywhere else in Mesopotamia (Woolley 1982, 87), which is a region and collection of cultures that many see as devoid of any beliefs in the afterlife. There are no Mesopotamian religious ritual texts, from any period or culture in the region, that concern life after death or how to transition to the afterlife as there are countless from Egypt during the same time period. The closest that any Mesopotamian written texts come to an articulation of the afterlife can be found in *The Epic of Gilgamesh*, but that text is a myth and not a ritual or guide for one to attain life after death (Sandars 1972, 30). With that said, the *Epic* takes the stance that immortality is not for mortals when the gods tell Gilgamesh that "everlasting life is not your destiny" (Sandars 1972, 70). All of this then makes the necropolis at Ur that much more important and mysterious.

The burials at Ur spanned a more than 2,000 year period, from the Early Dynastic Period until possibly the time of Alexander the Great (ca. 330 BCE), when Ur was finally abandoned (Porada 1960, 228). Woolley cleared about 2,000 burials of which he identified sixteen to be rulers or members of Ur's nobility (Woolley 1982, 54). Most of the graves were similar and consisted of a rectangular shaft that was between four and twelve feet deep, where the deceased was laid wrapped in matting or inside a coffin (Woolley 1982, 54). There was a range of materials that comprised the coffins and these included wood, basketwork, and even clay (Woolley 1982, 54). Although most of the burials pale in sophistication compared to those from Egypt, the fact that the graves exist at all seems to point towards a belief in the afterlife, but Woolley pointed out that nothing was ever discovered in the graves that would corroborate such an opinion. For instance, there were no religious symbols or ornaments found in the graves and there were no luxury items deposited there, which one would expect to take with on a journey to the afterlife (Woolley 1982, 55). With that said, there were two aspects of the graves of Ur that seem to point convincingly toward a belief in the afterlife.

The first aspect of the Ur burials that seems to point in a more well-developed belief in the afterlife is the elaborate ways in which some of the tombs were built. Many of the tombs were built of stone or burned mud-brick. Although many of the tombs consisted of a single chamber, some of the ones presumably made for the nobles were comprised of several rooms (Woolley 1982, 60). One can again use ancient Egypt as a corollary to understand the relation of tombs and the belief in the afterlife. Generally speaking, in ancient Egypt, the larger the tomb the more important the person was as he/she needed the room not only for his/her body, but also to house all of the luxury items needed in the afterlife. Despite some similarities in the size of the Ur tombs to those of Egypt, the similarities appear to end there, as no tombs from Ur had inscriptions on their walls, few luxury items have been discovered in them, and there are no signs that the people of Ur practiced mummification. Archaeologists know that the people of Ur did not practice mummification because a number of human remains have been found in the tombs, which leads to the second aspect of the tombs that can provide some details into the people of Ur's beliefs in the afterlife.

Perhaps the most fascinating, yet macabre aspect of the Ur necropolis is the existence of human sacrifice. In his excavations, Woolley discovered a surplus of human remains in some tombs, which he attributed to some sort of ritual of human sacrifice whereby nobles would take their servants with them after death (Woolley 1982, 60). Woolley pointed out that the number of sacrificed servants varied from tomb to tomb – from a half dozen to eighty – and that their existence along with the refilling of the tomb shaft was indicative of an elaborate religious ritual (Woolley 1982, 60). There is no evidence that children were sacrificed or that women followed their dead husbands as in the ancient Indian ritual of *sati* (Woolley 1982, 90). Most of the sacrificed victims appear to have been household servants in the case of the women, or armed guards when males could be identified (Woolley 1982, 91). A few items, such as lyres or harps, have been discovered in the tombs, but as stated above, the Ur tombs are quite barren compared to their Egyptian contemporaries. Since these were the tombs of nobles, the lack of material wealth cannot be given as the reason for the austere nature of the tombs. Of course tomb robbery, which was quite common in ancient Egypt, may be a factor for the Spartan accommodations in the Ur tombs, but unless more is revealed concerning such things, then it is pure conjecture. One of the best preserved of all the Ur tombs belonged to a woman known as Queen Puabi.

Among all the nameless tombs in the Ur necropolis one stands apart because its owner has been identified through some items that were recovered. The tomb, named by archaeologists as Tomb PG 800, belonged to a woman identified as Queen Puabi who lived in the third millennium BCE (Miller 2013, 127). The queen's name is known from three inscribed seals discovered in the chamber that bear her name along with the Sumerian title *nin*, which is normally taken to be the feminine equivalent of *lugal* used at Ur during the period to denote lordship (Woolley 1982, 88-89). Other names were discovered among the queen's tomb, as well as another royal tomb at Ur, but those particular individuals have not been definitively identified (Woolley 1982, 89). Queen Puabi's tomb offers modern scholars a plethora of interesting archaeological evidence, but little that helps to solve the problem of Mesopotamian views of the afterlife, but perhaps what is not said in the tombs of Ur may tell more than what is.

The existence of writing in the tombs of Ur was actually quite rare, as mentioned above; no inscriptions exist on any of the tomb walls, but its absence should be considered in its historical context. Generally speaking, throughout history, myths were transmitted for centuries orally before they were recorded in writing (Vansina 1985, 118). In the case of Ur and Mesopotamia in general, the greatest example of myth is of course the *Epic of Gilgamesh*, which is believed to have been first recorded in writing in the third millennium BCE (Sandars 1972, 7), or just around the time of Queen Puabi. It may be that writing at Ur, at least in terms of myth and ritual, had not yet advanced enough to make it into the tombs. With that said, it should be pointed out that myth and religious ritual were not necessarily inclusive in the ancient Near East, although there was considerable overlap as can be seen in ancient Egyptian rituals concerning the transition to the afterlife that had corollaries in myth. In the case of ancient Ur, the *Epic of Gilgamesh* provides modern scholars with the best example of early mythology, but as noted above, is lacking in ritual and seems to point against a Mesopotamian belief in the afterlife. It also needs to be stated that no copies of *Gilgamesh* have been discovered in any of the Ur tombs, which again, if present, could indicate a belief in the afterlife. Although *Gilgamesh* and other Sumerian myths lay clearly in the purview of myth and not ritual, some scholars believe that a more thorough investigation may help shed more light on the theological significance of the Ur necropolis.

One passage in particular from *Gilgamesh* where Gilgamesh's friend, Enkidu, has a vision of the afterlife, offers a possible glimpse into what the owners of the Ur tombs expected in the afterlife. The passage reads, "There is the house whose people sit in darkness; dust is their food and clay their meat. They are clothed like birds with wings for covering, they see no light, they sit in darkness. I entered the house of dust and I saw the king of the earth, their crowns put away forever; rulers and princes, all those who once wore kingly crowns and ruled the world in the days of old. They who had stood in the place of the gods like Anu and Enlil, stood now like servants to fetch baked meats in the house of dust, to carry cooked meat and cold water from the water-skin. In the house of dust which I entered were high priests and acolytes, priests of the incantation and of ecstasy; there were servers of the temple, and there was Etana, that king of Kish whom the eagle carried to heaven in the days of old. I saw also Samuqan, god of cattle, and there was Ereshkigal the Queen of the Underworld; and Belit-Sheri squatted in front of her, she who is recorder of the gods and keeps the book of death. She held a tablet from which she read. She raised her head, she saw me and spoke: 'Who has brought this one here?' (Sandars 1971, 92).

The Mesopotamian Underworld does not sound like a very inviting place; its description as a dark, dirty place sounds much like a tomb, which may not be coincidental. The necropolis of Ur was surely an important discovery whose secrets may at some future date be revealed, but unfortunately for the time being scholars are at an impasse concerning its ritual and theological importance. Excavations at Ur have also uncovered another important religious institution that fortunately more is known about.

In the ancient Near East, religion was a complex affair where hundreds or even thousands of gods and goddesses were recognized and worshipped by any single group of people. Many of these deities had very small followings, but the more important ones were attended to by priests and priestesses who sometimes amassed great power. At Ur the most important of all deities was the divine pair of Nanna and Ningal. Nanna was the Sumerian god of the Moon, who later became better known by his Semitic name Sin, and his divine consort was Ningal. According to Sumerian mythology, their most notable offspring was the sun god Utu, known more commonly by the Semitic Shamash, who wed the Mesopotamian goddess of love and war, Ishtar (Sandars 1972, 122-24). Since Nanna and Ningal occupied the prime position in the spiritual life of Ur, the city's large temple complex was dedicated to the pair and along with it a loyal following of priests and priestesses.

The Sumerian word for the priests of the Ur III Dynasty was *en* and the accompanying female equivalent for priestess was *entu*. Evidence, in the form of administrative documents, reveals that the *en* priests exercised immense political and economic power not just in Ur, but throughout southern Mesopotamia (Sharlach 2007, 70). The *entu* priestesses also wielded as much, if not more, power and were quite influential in Ur's religious life during and after the Ur III Dynasty. Since religion was intertwined with all aspects of life in ancient Mesopotamia, any person with an important religious position held great influence in Ur. In fact, the *entu* priestesses of Ur were viewed as so important to the city's cultural integrity that subsequent dynasties that conquered Ur continued to patronize the religious institution, as will be demonstrated below.

The *entu* priestess at Ur lived in a special section of the Nanna-Ningal temple complex called the *giparu*. Although the priestesses lived in the *giparu*, it was not a cloistered life and evidence shows that they took part in everyday city life just like other inhabitants of Ur (Sharlach 2007, 70). Besides housing the priestesses, the *giparu* was also the location where the women carried out the day to day rituals associated with the cult (Weadock 1975, 101). The woman who was appointed as the head priestess, or *entu*, enjoyed immense power while she held the title, but also had many responsibilities to carry out such as the day to day functions mentioned above and to some extent the political will of the person who appointed her. The priestesses of the *giparu* were specially chosen for the important role and had to be of royal blood, which during the Ur III Dynasty usually meant they had to be the daughter or sister of the king (Weadock 1975, 101). Performing the day to day rituals was important, but the true theological value of the priestesses at the *giparu* of Ur was more symbolic; the women were seen as and believed to be the human wives of the god Nanna and therefore filled the temporal role as Ningal (Weadock 1975, 101). The use of female priestesses as intermediaries for a divine marriage was not unknown in the ancient Near East – the ancient Egyptians had a religious institution similar to the *giparu* known as the God's Wife of Amun – but the women of the *giparu* at Ur are the oldest known cases in the world. The priestesses of the *giparu* usually did their work away from public eyes (1975, 103). After the Ur III Dynasty, during what is known as the First Isin Dynasty (ca. 2017-1739 BCE) and the Larsa Dynasty (ca. 1793-1763 BCE), a sub-cult within the Nanna-Ningal complex developed where the dead *entus* were worshipped (Weadock 1975, 104). The *giparu* and the priestesses who lived there were truly an integral part of Ur's religious life, but they also played a role in the economics and politics of the city.

Archaeological excavations at Ur have revealed that the actual *giparu* building went through a process several times – beginning as early as the Early Dynastic Period and continuing until the Neo-Babylonian Period – where the structure was built, destroyed, and rebuilt (Weadock 1975, 101). The fact that the building and its cult was given so much attention in different periods and by different dynasties indicates that it served as an important political focal point as much as it did a religious one. Although some form of the *giparu* may have existed at Ur as early as the Early Dynastic Period, it was during the Ur III Dynasty when it acquired its true political power. The building was added to, or perhaps an entirely new one was built, during the reign of Ur-Nammu and it was in his successors' reigns that patronage of the cult acquired political significance (Weadock 1975, 107). Among the ways that the *entu* priestesses were able to wield their power was through the vast estates that were owned by Nanna and Ningal and therefore the *giparu* (Weadock 1975, 103). In the ancient Near East most land was owned by either the king or the various gods and goddesses of a particular kingdom and since the deities could not physically collect taxes and payments for using their lands, the priests and priestesses of their cults would. Since the cults of Nanna and Ningal were the most important at Ur, their cult was the wealthiest. The influence that emanated from the *giparu* at Ur lasted for hundreds of years, but was not without interruptions. Archaeological work on the building has revealed that it suffered a particularly costly and destructive setback when the Elamites attacked and sacked Ur, which ended the Ur III Dynasty (Weadock 1975, 107).

Chapter 6: The End of the Ur III Dynasty and the Temporary Destruction of Ur

As strong as the Ur III state was, it was not successful in its attempts to placate other peoples to the east of Mesopotamia. In particular, a group of people called the Elamites burst onto the scene in Mesopotamia; later the Elamites would be responsible for building their own kingdoms complete with impressive works of art and architecture, but around 2000 BCE they were purely interested in plunder. Besides the archaeological evidence that shows a great destruction level at Ur concurrent with the end of the Ur III state, numerous cuneiform texts were compiled at later dates that lamented the destruction of Ur. One of the more well-known texts reads, "His righteous city which has been destroyed – bitter is its lament. His Ur which has been destroyed – bitter is its lament. They lament which is bitter – O city, set up thy lament . . . The Subarians and the Elamites, the destroyers made of it thirty shekels. The righteous house they break up with the pickaxe; the people groan. The city they make into ruins; the people groan. Its lady cries: 'Alas for my city,' cries: 'Alas for my house." Ningal cries: 'Alas for my city,' cries" Alas for my house.' As for me, the woman, my city has been destroyed, my house too has been destroyed; O Nanna, Ur has been destroyed, its people have been dispersed." (Pritchard 1992, 455-461).

In terms of historiography, the text is important because it places much of the blame for Ur's destruction at the hands of the Elamites, who were actually ruled by a kingdom called Shimashki, which is referred to in the text as the Subarians (Van de Mieroop 2007, 83). The text is also important archeologically, as it corroborates destruction discovered at Ur in the form of burn layers, and also theologically. The theological implications of Ur's destruction will be considered more below, but the causes that led to the city's decline must be considered.

Although the Elamites and Subarians are attributed with being the cause of the destruction of the city of Ur and the Ur III Dynasty, a number of factors precipitated the decline. History demonstrates that strong societies are always able to repel invaders, especially when they are less advanced technologically, so in order to understand Ur's destruction one must consider internal factors within Ur III society. Modern scholars point out that one of Ur's greatest strengths, its economy, also ended up being part of its decline to a certain extent. As efficient as the Ur III economy was in regards to the outlying provinces who paid tribute to Ur, those same provinces often operated independently and sometimes with Ur's enemies (Van de Mieroop 2007, 82). The confederated nature of Ur III's economy seemed to work well when the state was strong, but the constituent parts that made up the whole were not willing to help when Ur was threatened. By the time of the last Ur III king, Ibbi-Sin (ca. 2028-2004), many of the outlying provinces had begun to assert their political as well as their economic independence.

The political problems in the Ur III Dynasty probably began during the rule of Shu-Sin (ca. 2037-2029), but reached crisis proportions during Ibbi-Sin's rule (Kuhrt 2010, 1:70). Several provinces quit paying their taxes to Ur and scribes in some of the more important cities under Ur's control – Umma, Girsu, and Nippur – quit dating documents under Ibbi-Sin's name (Van de Mieroop 2007, 82). Dating and chronology in the ancient Near East was done according to king lists and annals and like most other things during the period was intertwined with religion. The king of Ur was appointed by the gods so when the scribes quit using their names to date documents, it demonstrates that the other cities of Mesopotamia began to lose respect for Ur's political leaders.

A correspondence letter between two members of the Ur III bureaucracy summarizes the political situation: "After you have spoken to Ibbi-Sin, my king: 'This is what Isbi-Erra, your servant, says: 'I was ordered to buy barley. The barley has a value of 1 (sheqel silver) per kor of barley (and) 20 talents of silver have been provided for the barley-purchase. Reports were received that hostile Martu (Amorites) entered your territory and I have brought 72,000 kor of barley, the entire barley, into Isin. Now the Martu have completely penetrated into the land of Sumer (and) have captured all the fortresses there. Because of the Martu I cannot give the barley to be threshed. They are stronger than I. I should be seized. May my king have 600 transport boats of 120 kor capacity be prepared . . . I shall assume (protection of) the place where the boats dock, and thus all (?) the barley may be stored (and) transferred in its totality. Assuming that you let the barley diminish too much, I shall have barley brought in to you. My king, the Elamite has become bitter in battle, his barley-rations will soon be finished, you should not let (the strength of) your arm grow slack, you should not hasten to enter a servant-relationship with him, and you should not run after him! Barley for 15 years: your provisions of the palace and the city are all in my hand. The guarding of Isian and Nibru my king, I am taking upon myself! May my king know (this)!'" (Kuhrt 2010: 1:70-71).

The lack of grain put Ibbi-Sin and Ur in a precarious position, not because the king was unable to feed his people, but because he was unable to pay his troops to protect the city. Why Ur lacked in grain at this period is unclear; it may have to do with outlying states that asserted their independence and refused to pay the grain taxes, or there may have been a famine or drought (Van de Mieroop 2007, 83), or more than likely there were a number of factors that contributed. The search for answers as to why Ur declined seem to lead only to more questions, but later inhabitants of Ur clearly placed the blame on their predecessors.

Most of the extant cuneiform texts that relate to the destruction of Ur are replete with theological references. In most of these texts it is either implied, or stated quite explicitly that Ur suffered because its inhabitants failed to worship the Sumerian deities properly. One text reads:

> "That kingship be carried off from the land,
>
> That its face be directed to inimical soil,
>
> That in accord with the command of An (and)
>
> Enlil, 'law and order' cease to exist –
>
> (All this was) after An had frowned upon all the
>
> Lands,
>
> After Enlil had set his (friendly) face to inimical
>
> Soil,
>
> After Nintu had prostrated her (own) creatures,
>
> After Enki had overturned (the course of) the Tigris
>
> (and) Euphrates,
>
> After Utu had cursed the roads (and highways . . .
>
> An, Enlil, Enki, (and) Ninhursag decreed (as) its fate –
>
> The fate decreed by them cannot be changed . . .
>
> Enlil brought down Elam, the foe, form the mountain,
>
> He made Nanshe, the princely daughter, dwell in
>
> a strange city,
>
> He put Ninmar to the flames in (her) shrine
>
> Gubba,
>
> Its silver (and) lapus lazuli is carried off in big boats . . .
>
> On Hursagkalamma, the house of Kish, an evil hand

Was placed . . .

Before Enlil a lament was set up in his city, the shrine

Nippur . . .

Girsu, the city of heroes, was turned into a cowardly

Place . . .

Oh Enki, your city has been cursed, it has been made

into enemy territory,

Why do you reckon us among those who have been

displaced from Eridu . . .

Below, the Elamites like those who bring forth

Woe, brandish their weapons,

Above, like chaff blown about by the wind, the

Steppe . . .

Ur, the great wild ox that (formerly) stepped forth

Confidently (in combat), has been made prostrate." (Pritchard 1992, 612-19).

Few if any scholars today would argue that the Sumerian gods played a direct role in Ur's decline, but it would be logical to assume that along with the other problems Ur experienced, a general lack of religious feeling in the city contributed to an overall cultural malaise. Once the inhabitants of Ur quit caring out their religion, they also quit caring about their leaders, government, and other cultural traditions, which eventually allowed foreign invaders to easily overrun the city.

After the Elamites overran and sacked Ur, they captured Ibbi-Sin and brought the unlucky king back to Elam. The Elamites then occupied Ur for about seven years until a king from the city of Isin named Ishbi-Erra (ca. 2017-1985 BCE) drove out the intruders (Van de Mieroop 2007, 84). Mesopotamia then reverted to a political situation that was very similar to the circumstances before the ascendancy of the Ur III Dynasty – fragmentation and competing city-states (Kuhrt 2010, 1:74). Among the cities that grew in power during this period were Babylon, Mari, Isin, and Larsa; Ur survived but its political power was for the most part eliminated. The golden age of Ur's hegemony over Mesopotamia was gone, but its cultural and political importance continued to endure.

According to the Sumerian King List, Ishbi-Erra, the king of Isin who drove the Elamites from Ur, began his political career as an official under the last king of Ur III, Ibbi-Sin (Kuhrt 2010, 1:76). Although Ishbi-Erra ruled his kingdom from Isin and is acknowledged by modern scholars as the first king of the Isin Dynasty and therefore distinct from Ur III, he practiced a program of cultural continuity that connected Isin with Ur. For instance, he retained many of the royal titulary and epithets used by the kings of Ur III, such as "king of the four quarters of the Universe" and he patronized the *giparu* of Ur (Kuhrt 2010, 1:76). In terms of the *giparu*, after Ishbi-Erra established himself as king of Isin and assumed control over Ur, he retained Ibbi-Sin's daughter as the *entu* priestess until her death and then he kept the tradition by installing his own daughter (Kuhrt 2010, 1:76). Despite Ishbi-Erra's patronage of Ur's religious institutions and his use of the city's royal ideology, subsequent Isin kings began to ignore Ur and finally Isin was itself overtaken by the city of Larsa. Despite these unfortunate turn of events, Ur's importance in Mesopotamia would endure.

Chapter 7: Ur's Revival under the Kassites and Babylonians

Although Larsa may have been the immediate victor of its struggle with Isin for control over southern Mesopotamia, it was Babylon that ultimately took home most of the spoils. Under what modern scholars refer to as the First Dynasty of Babylon, also sometimes known as the Amorite Dynasty, Babylon became a world class city under rulers such as Hammurabi (ca. 1792-1750), who is known for his violent conquest of most of Mesopotamia and his eponymous law code (Van de Mieroop 2007, 111-15). The great kings of Babylon dedicated most of their building activities to their own city and so Ur was once more relegated to a backwater, which was aggravated even further when Mesopotamia entered a dark age around 1590 BCE that lasted for about 100 years (Van de Mieroop 2007, 122-23). During the Mesopotamian Dark Age Babylon suffered extensive damage, but when the smoke finally cleared, it was ruled by a new dynasty known as the Kassites who continued many Mesopotamian traditions, which included taking a renewed interest in Ur.

Mesopotamian history was one of competing cities and dynasties, which, as evidenced by Ur's destruction at the hands of the Elamites, was often violent. With that said, the numerous ethnicities of Mesopotamia often worshipped the same deities and so respect and observance of a city's religious temples and institutions was usually given by conquering kings. Temples that were destroyed were often rebuilt and the ones that were not ruined were often given additions. When the Kassites took control of Babylon, they went to great lengths to portray themselves as legitimate Babylonian rulers by doing things such as returning the statue of the god Marduk to its temple in the city (Kuhrt 2010, 1:338) and using the Sumerian and Akkadian languages in religious and administrative documents (Kuhrt 2010, 1:339). The Kassites also took an interest in Ur's religious institutions.

Around the year 1400 BCE, the Kassite-Babylonian king Kurigalzu I embarked on a program to rebuild many of the religious sanctuaries of Ur (Weadock 1975, 111). The precise reason for this program remains unknown because there are a lack of written sources that detail the work, but it would follow the efforts of political legitimatization that the other Kassites undertook at Babylon. The interesting aspect of Kurigalzu's efforts in Ur though is that the projects appear to have taken a more secular character (Clayden 1995, 63). In particular, the *giparu*, which played such an important role during the Ur III Dynasty, was retained as a residential area but was no longer part of the Ningal Temple (Clayden 1995, 63). The Ningal Temple was moved to the ziggurat terrace away from the *giparu*, which indicates a weakening of the power of the *entu* priestesses, but not necessarily of Ur itself. After the re-founding of the Ningal Temple by the Kassite kings, subsequent dynasties did little to maintain the temple or patronize its cults and so the temple complex fell into decay and the office of the *entu* disappeared until the seventh century BCE (Clayden 1995, 63).

One of the most impressive aspects of the Kassites was their ability to prolong their rule over Mesopotamia and endure in a way that no other dynasty was able to do before them. The Kassites ruled the region from around 1530 to 1155 BCE, which would certainly make them among the longest ruling dynasties of the ancient Near East (Kuhrt 2010, 1:335). The period of Kassite control over Ur took place when the kings of Babylon vied with those from Egypt, Hatti, and Assyria for control over their lesser neighbors. The great powers usually avoided direct confrontations with one another and instead preferred diplomacy to settle their differences (Kuhrt 2010, 1:339), but by the twelfth century BCE the Assyrians had become the dominant power in Mesopotamia. The warlike Assyrians destroyed and conquered many cities in the ancient Near East and Ur, which was ancient when they came to power, was usually a part of their imperial plans.

Chapter 8: The Assyrians and Ur

Although Ur was located far from Assyria, which was to the north near the headwaters of the Tigris River, it was still an important symbolic city in Mesopotamia when the Assyrians began their conquest of Mesopotamia in the twelfth century. Despite being particularly warlike people, the Assyrians were also quite literate and adept at historical writing. It was during the reign of the Assyrian king Tiglath-Pileser I (ca. 1114-1076) that the Assyrians first began to record their military expeditions, royal hunts, and building programs in detailed chronological annals (Van de Mieroop 2007, 180). The context of the annals was theological in nature as they were meant to be letters from the kings to their gods (Speiser 1983, 66), but much geographic and historical information can be gleaned from them if one can discern myth from history. With that said, when Tiglath-Pileser I began recording his historical deeds for his gods, the city of Ur was listed as one of the ones under his control. The annals state: "Arpadda, Haurâni . . . ——ta——, Dinanu, [Kaprabi,] cities of Bit-Adinia, Ta—ri . . . Hrumu, Anlama—, Urrus, Ur." (Luckenbill, 1:294). The reference demonstrates that although Ur may have been relegated once more to backwater status, it still retained some it its luster, at least enough for the mighty Assyrian king to mention it among his conquests.

Ur figured more prominently in the annals of later Assyrian kings and also in construction programs. Sargon II (721-705 BCE) mentioned Ur in a couple of different annals as one of the cities that he "reestablished" by returning its cult statues – referred to simply as "gods" in the texts – that had been taken away by previous conquerors. The text reads, "The people of Sippar, Nippur, Babylon, Borsippa, who were imprisoned therein through no fault of theirs, - I broke their bonds and caused them to behold the light (of day). Their fields, which since days of old, during the anarchy in the land, the Sutu had seized, I returned to them. The Sutu, desert folk, I cut down with the sword. Their borders, which had been encroached upon, I restored to their former limits. The independence of Ur, Erech, Eridu, Larsa, Kisik and Nimid-Laguda, I (re)established, and brought back their captured gods to their cities. Their revenues, which had stopped, I restored." (Luckenbill, 2:20-1).

Another annal from Sargon II's reign also lists Ur as one of the cities of the Assyrian Empire, but notes that the Assyrian king had to "quiet" its people, which points towards a rebellion. The text states, "I undertook the (re)habilitation of Sippar, Nippur, Babylon and Borsippa, I made good the losses of client people, all there were, and remitted the taskwork of Der, Ur, Uruk, Eridu, Larsa, Kullab, Kissik, and Nimid-Laguda, I quieted their people. The freedom of Assur and Harran, which from distant days had been overlooked and their clientship, which had ceased, I restored." (Luckenbill, 2:101).

The rebellion that was inferred in the text is further corroborated by a text from the reign of the Assyrian king Sennacherib (704-681 BCE). Sennacherib carried on the same violent program of conquest that Sargon II did, but the annals that the king left behind are more revealing of the political situation. One particular annal from Sennacherib's reign details a war that he fought against the king of Babylon and his allies, among which was Ur. The annal said, "At the beginning of my reign, when I solemnly took my seat on the throne, and ruled the inhabitants of Assyria with mercy and grace, Merodach-Baladan, king of Babylonia, and instigator of revolt, plotter of rebellion, doer of evil, whose guilt is heavy, brought over to his side Shutur-Nahundu, the Elamite, and gave him gold, silver and precious stones, and secured him as an ally. Imbappa, *turtan* of the king of Elam, Tannânu, the second in command, 10 (division) commanders, together with Nergal-nâsir, the Sutean, who was fearless in battle, 80,000 bowmen, . . . horses which were with them, he sent to Sumer and Akkad (Babylonia) to his aid. And that [Merodach-Baladan], the cities of . . . Ur, Eridu, Kullab, Kissik, Nimid-Laguda, the lands of Bit-Iakin, Bit-Amukkâni, Bit-Salli, Bit-Dakkuri, all the Chaldeans . . . all of Babylonia, he gathered together and marshaled for the fight. (Luckenbill, 2:128-9).

A depiction of Sennacherib located in his palace

Although it is known that Sennacherib was able to successfully reconquer most of Mesopotamia, it is not known what, if any, repercussions he leveled on Ur. At this point it is unknown if Sennacherib ordered widespread destruction to Ur, as per the Assyrian practice towards those who resisted them, but it is known that one of his successors dedicated considerable resources to the southern Mesopotamian city.

The Assyrians were known to generally be cruel towards cities and peoples who resisted them, often moving entire populations of those who resisted them to the far corners of their empire. The forced removal of resistive populations took place after the mighty Assyrian army destroyed the city, or cities, in question by leveling the buildings and capturing the cult statues of their most important gods and goddesses. Ashurbanipal (668-627 BCE), who was one of the last kings of the neo-Assyrian Dynasty, is viewed by many today as being one of the kings who employed these brutal tactics more than most and certainly more widespread than his predecessors. Ashurbanipal destroyed numerous Mesopotamian cities along with others in the Levant and Egypt, which certainly made him more prolific than many of his ancestors in terms of destruction, but evidence also reveals that he took an interest in Ur.

Most of the references that Assyrian kings made to Ur took place in the context of conquest or rebellion, but Ashurbanipal referenced the ancient city in a religious text where he sought to please his gods. The text reads, "The great gods in their council decreed (for me) a favorable destiny, and granted (me) a receptive mind. They caused me to grasp all of the scribal art. In the assembly of princes, [they magnified] my name, they made my rule powerful. Might, virility, enormous power, they granted me; the unsubmissive lands they placed in my hands. They caused me to attain unto the priesthood [which I desired]. The offerings I brought were pleasing to [the gods]. The sanctuaries of the great gods, my lords [I restored] with gold and [silver]. Colossi, storm-bird images and mighty columns I set up by their gates. [Esharra], Emashmash, the temple of the Lady of the land . . ., [I made splendid] like the [heavenly 'writing.'] The Lady . . . over . . . the land Ur." (Luckenbill, 2:323-24).

The text clearly references improvements that Ashurbanipal made at Ur, which would indicate that the city was still theologically important in the seventh century BCE. Archeological work done at Ur by Woolley and later examined by other scholars seems to corroborate Ashurbanipal's claims.

As noted above, the *giparu* of Ur was built, rebuilt, expanded, and moved on several occasions during different dynasties. What the *giparu* and the *entu* priestesses that served there meant to the different dynasties varied, but they all saw the institution and the deities Nanna and Ningal as important theological and political pillars of Ur. The Assyrian governor Sin-balassu-iqbi, who served under Ashurbanipal, rebuilt the *giparu* near its original location around 650 BCE, but did not re-install the office of the *entu* priestess (Weadock 1975, 112). It is unknown why Ashurbanipal did not re-install the office, but one can assume that since the king was so active with military conquests, which he led personally, he did not have the time to install one of his daughters as per the tradition. Other evidence excavated from Ur that can be definitively dated to the neo-Assyrian Dynasty, such as a large horde of jewelry from a central treasury (Reade 2001, 178), indicates that Ur had a certain level of material wealth and possible influence in the later periods of ancient Mesopotamian history. The Assyrian period discoveries at Ur demonstrate once more the continued importance of the city and Ashurbanipal's activity there was one of continuity with previous dynasties and once the Assyrians were toppled in quick order, Ur continued to impress kings and was inhabited by a sizable population.

Chapter 9: Ur in Later Ancient Times

As dynasties and people rose and fell throughout the ancient Near East, Ur was one of the constants; it suffered destruction at the hands of invaders and was neglected from time to time, but it always seemed to reemerge to inspire a new dynasty. After the Assyrians were ultimately vanquished from the political and cultural chessboard of Mesopotamia, a new dynasty quickly stepped in to fill their place – the Neo-Babylonian Dynasty. As the name indicates, the Neo-Babylonians based their dynasty out of the venerable city of Babylon, but they were outsiders as they were members of a Semitic ethnic group known as the Chaldeans who migrated to the region around Babylon in the early first millennium BCE (Kuhrt 2010, 2:275). The best known of all Neo-Babylonian kings was Nebuchadnezzar II (604-562 BCE) from the numerous references to him in the Old Testament, but it was the last Neo-Babylonian king, Nabonidus (555-539 BCE), who dedicated resources towards the preservation of Ur and its culture.

The reign of Nabonidus is particularly well documented as there are a number of extant texts that chronicle the king's rise and ultimate fall at the hands of the Achaemenid Persians. According to some of the texts, Ur was among a number of other cities in southern Mesopotamia that had fallen into ruin and decadence, which the king set right personally. The text said, "But the citizens of Babylon, Borsippa, Nippur, Ur, Uruk (and) Larsa, the administrators (and) the inhabitants of the urban centers of Babylonia acted evil, careless and even sinned against his great divine power, having not (yet) experienced the awfulness of the wrath of the Divine Crescent, the king of all gods; they disregarded his rites and there was much irreligious and disloyal talk. They devoured one another like dogs, caused disease and hunger to appear among them. . . For ten years I was moving around among these (cities) and did not enter my own city Babylon." (Pritchard 1992, 562).

A depiction of Nabonidus

The text appears to operate on two different levels: there is the formulaic aspect of the text where the citizens of Ur invited their ruin through their own follies – which is similar to the texts that described the city's fall at the end of the Ur III Dynasty – and there is the historiographical component that states Nabonidus visited each of the cities in southern Mesopotamia. It is not known how long Nabonidus stayed in Ur, but the evidence shows that he made at least nominal efforts to consolidate his power in the city.

The most notable political maneuver that Nabonidus made in Ur was to revive the office of *entu*. As noted above, the *entu* priestesses wielded considerable power in Ur and although the *giparu* was rebuilt during the reign of Ashurbanipal, the office itself remained vacant. In true Ur religious tradition Nabonidus appointed his daughter, Ennigaldi-Nanna, as the head priestess (Weadock 1975, 101), which no doubt gave the king eyes and ears all over the city. In fact, it seems as though Nabonidus' re-installation of the office of the *entu* priestess was more of a practical matter than for any deep veneration of Ur and its traditions. Nabonidus' grip over Mesopotamia was tenuous at best, so in order to bring the still important city of Ur firmly under his control, he had to gain control of one of the city's most important religious institutions. Despite his best efforts, Nabonidus was vanquished from the throne when the Achaemenid Persian king, Cyrus led his army into Babylon and although the Achaemenids dedicated most of their resources to the larger cities in their empire, evidence shows that Ur endured under their rule.

Excavations from Ur have revealed that the top or latest archaeological level of private residences can be dated definitively to the Persian period (Porada 1960, 228). A number of coins were also discovered at the same level in what is believed to have been a seal cutter's workshop (Porada 1960, 230). The coins demonstrate that Ur continued as a residence after the Persians conquered Mesopotamia, but they do not reveal how important the city was to the Persians. The coins show a plethora of different artistic influences – Greek, Egyptian, Babylonian, Assyrian, and Persian – and most are dated, which means that a terminal date for Ur's occupation can be surmised. Based on the numismatic evidence, along with extant tablets, Ur was probably deserted sometime after Alexander the Great's conquest of the region around 331 BCE (Porada 1960, 228). After Ur was abandoned, it was over 2,000 years until scholars and adventurers re-discovered the city and all its glories. But Ur's desertion and its modern re-discovery are not the final chapter in the city's rich history; more recently Ur has struggled to survive amid great political turmoil.

Chapter 10: Ur's Modern Struggle for Existence

Pictures of Americans walking among the ruins of Ur

The final chapter in Ur's long and venerable history is still being written and because of the instability in the region, it hangs precariously in the winds and is to be determined by the capricious nature of those who care little about the city's ancient mysteries. When Saddam Hussein took power over Iraq, he invited scholars from all over the world to come to his country to study and preserve its ancient Mesopotamian monuments. In this respect Hussein could be said to be a patron of ancient Mesopotamian history, but the dictator also brought destruction to those monuments through incessant warfare.

Hussein involved Iraq in three wars that were extremely costly in terms of human lives, the country's infrastructure, and the perhaps less well-known destruction to the country's ancient antiquities. From 1980-88 Iraq fought Iran in a particularly brutal and bloody war and then was invaded in 1991 during Operation Desert Storm and again in 2003, which of course was a much longer war that continues to this day to some extent with the fight against the Islamic State in the northern part of the country. Minimal damage to the country's antiquities was incurred during the Iraq-Iran war, but major theft and looting of museum pieces – many of which came from Ur – and indirect attacks took place on Ur and other ancient sites during the wars in 1991 and 2003 (Schipper 2005, 251).

The American led coalition's invasion of Iraq in 1991 may have seemed orderly to those who watched the live events on CNN, but the results were a bit more chaotic, especially in terms of Iraq's ancient antiquities. The Iraq Antiquities Authority estimated that approximately 4,000 items were stolen from its museums (Schipper 2015, 252). Many of the pieces looted from the museums ended up in private collections in Europe and North America, which were apparently "ordered" by unscrupulous individuals before the invasion began (Schipper 2005, 252). During the invasion, Ur took several hits from missiles and gunfire; most notably the Ziggurat of Ur took a direct hit and was left with approximately 400 shell holes on its southern wall (Schipper 2005, 252-2). There were also five large bomb craters visible near the ziggurat, which for a time served as an Iraqi military base (Schipper 2005, 254). The practice of using an ancient site as a military base was not new to the Iraqis as they also used the site of Babylon, which was then turned into a U.S. camp after the Americans invaded Iraq once more in 2003 (Schipper 2005, 255). Fortunately, the royal necropolis of Ur was left untouched by the vicissitudes of war even though they are as exposed as the ziggurat (Schipper 2005, 261).

Perhaps the biggest problem that Ur faced during this time was a lack of professional scholars who could have mitigated the damage done by war. Between 1991 and 2003 few non-Iraqi scholars visited the country and those who did only did so between 1999 and 2003 (Schipper 2005, 253). The archaeological situation in Iraq in general and specifically at Ur further deteriorated after the invasion of 2003 (Schipper 2005, 270). With the current Iraqi government barely able to contain the Islamic State in the north, Ur's archaeological future hangs in limbo.

A modern aerial view of Ur

Ruins of a floor and walls in one of the buildings in Ur

Online Resources

Other books about ancient history by Charles River Editors

Other books about the Sumerians on Amazon

Other books about Ur on Amazon

Other books about Uruk on Amazon

Bibliography

Baker, H.D. "The Urban Landscape in First Millennium BC Babylonia". University of Vienna.

Beaulieu, Paul-Alain (2003). The Pantheon of Uruk During the Neo-Babylonian Period. BRILL. p. 424. ISBN 90-04-13024-1.

Charvát, Petr; Zainab Bahrani; Marc Van de Mieroop (2002). Mesopotamia Before History.

London: Routledge. p. 281. ISBN 0-415-25104-4.

Crawford, Harriet E. W. (2004). Sumer and the Sumerians. Cambridge University Press. p. 252. ISBN 0-521-53338-4.

Fassbinder, Jörg W. E.; Becker, Helmut; van Ess, Margarete (2003). "Magnetometry at Uruk (Iraq): the city of king Gilgamesh". Geophysical Research Abstracts. European Geophysical Society. 5 (9152): 1. Bibcode:2003EAEJA.....9152F. Retrieved 2009. Check date values in: |access-date= (help)

Harmansah, Ömür (2007-12-03). "The Archaeology of Mesopotamia: Ceremonial centers, urbanization and state formation in Southern Mesopotamia". Retrieved 2011-08-28.

Oppenheim, A. Leo; Erica Reiner (1977). Ancient Mesopotamia: Portrait of a Dead Civilization. Chicago: University of Chicago Press. p. 445. ISBN 0-226-63187-7

Chisholm, Hugh, ed. (1911). "Erech". Encyclopædia Britannica. 9 (11th ed.). Cambridge University Press. pp. 734–735.

Green, MW (1984). "The Uruk Lament". Journal of the American Oriental Society. 104 (2): 253–279. doi:10.2307/602171. JSTOR 602171.

Kuhrt, Amélie (1995). The Ancient Near East. London: Routledge. p. 782. ISBN 0-415-16763-9.

Liverani, Mario; Zainab Bahrani; Marc Van de Mieroop (2006). Uruk: The First City. London: Equinox Publishing. p. 97. ISBN 1-84553-191-4.

Lloyd, Seton (1955). Foundations in the Dust. New York, New York: Penguin Books. p. 217. ISBN 0-500-05038-4.

Postgate, J.N. (1994). Early Mesopotamia, Society and Economy at the Dawn of History. New York, New York: Routledge Publishing. p. 367. ISBN 0-415-00843-3.

Rothman, Mitchell S. (2001). Uruk, Mesopotamia & Its Neighbors. Santa Fe: School of American Research Press. p. 556. ISBN 1-930618-03-4.

Vos, Howard F. (1977). Archaeology in Bible Lands. Chicago, Illinois: Moody Press. p. 399. ISBN 978-0-8024-0293-6.

Free Books by Charles River Editors

We have brand new titles available for free most days of the week. To see which of our titles are currently free, click on this link.

Discounted Books by Charles River Editors

We have titles at a discount price of just 99 cents everyday. To see which of our titles are currently 99 cents, click on this link.

Printed in Dunstable, United Kingdom